Help, Drowning!

THROW ME A ROPE!

by

Margaret A. Wolf

PRESS

Introduction

My life was nearly snuffed out as a young child in a river near home. Many times and in many ways throughout my life, I have felt emotionally like I was drowning in my circumstances. I've felt overwhelmed and inadequate for the demands made of me. I've been in turmoil, in distress and overpowering grief. But through it all God has revealed Himself to me in ever expanding ways, and has shown Himself ready to meet me at my point of need. He has delivered me from rejection, and from all kinds of fear. He has healed me emotionally, physically, and spiritually. He has worked miracles in my family to restore relationships I had almost destroyed. He has walked me through the death of one of our sons. He's called me to heal the broken hearted, lift up the downtrodden, and set the captives free. He's prepared me for a life of service in which I earnestly desire to bring glory and honor to His name. This book is written as a testimony to God's goodness and mercy in my life.

As I've waded through my memories to write this book, I've marveled at the many different ways God has shown Himself strong on behalf of me and my family. Through all my adventures along the way, as we've moved around the world and back, I've gotten to know Him better and better. My prayer is that you will see, as you read this book, some of the ways God works in the lives of His children, both openly and behind the scenes. I pray that you will understand that God is no respecter of persons, but He will do for you what He has done for me. He desires to reveal Himself to you also, and will make Himself known to the same degree that <u>you</u> desire to know <u>Him</u> and choose to trust and obey Him. He says in His word *"Come near to God and he will come near to you"* (James 4:8).

I pray you will be encouraged to believe that God cares about your problems, whether big or small, and that He still works in mysterious — and sometimes miraculous — ways to show Himself strong on our behalf. I pray that you will find encouragement to hang in there and continue to seek after God in all <u>your</u> circumstances. God says to us, as He said to the children of Israel immediately after He had sent them into exile in Babylon: *"'For I know the plans I have for you,' declares the LORD, 'plans to prosper you and not to harm you, plans to give you hope and a future. Then you will call upon me and come and pray to me, and I will listen to you. You will seek me and find me when you seek me with all your heart.'"* (Jeremiah 29:11-13)

Acknowledgments

I wish to thank my friend Jean Norment for allowing God to use her to dramatically change my life. If she had not been available and willing to be used, I don't know how I could have survived many challenges that have come my way since then. But also, I would have missed out on a marvelous, exciting way of living, with God in control of my life.

I wish to thank Alice Holland who has always supported me in prayer and was my greatest mentor on this new walk of faith. I would also like to thank all my many friends in Aglow who have prayed faithfully for me and helped me to grow in the knowledge and understanding of God, and His gifts of the Spirit.

I wish to thank my husband John, who has stuck with me through thick and thin, and has been my friend and confidant, and my supporter in trying to fulfill God's call on my life.

I want to thank Lydia Burns who spent many hours pouring over my manuscript to help me with the editing.

And most of all, I continually thank God for setting me free from a prison of my own making — for breaking my heart of stone and giving me a heart of love for Him and for others. I thank Him for revealing and extending to me more of His grace than I could ever hope to deserve. I thank Him for permitting me to be a very tiny part of His Kingdom plan on earth.

Contents

CHAPTER ONE

Turning Point

"Lord, what's wrong with me? Why can't I seem to 'flow' with your Spirit? Why can't I hear your voice or move in the gifts of the Spirit like others do? What is it that's hindering me? If this blockage is something I need to deal with, show me what it is and what I need to do. If I don't need to deal with it, would you please just take it away?"

This was my prayer as I drove over to the hotel to pick up my friend Jean. On the previous day she had prayed for me to receive the "Baptism in the Holy Spirit," an experience that I had longed for and had asked God for on many occasions previously. But once again, I had felt no change, no difference. On this cool morning, in January 1982, Jean was going to be the guest teacher of the Bible study I had been teaching for a year and a half.

At that same moment, in her hotel room, Jean Norment was seeking the Lord about our Bible study and the needs of the women who attended.

As we drove around Washington's Capitol Beltway on our way to the home of our hostess, Jean began to share a few things the Lord had revealed to her: "God showed me somebody drowning. Someone in that Bible study nearly drowned at some point in her life."

Having been counseling the women in that class for a long time, I began searching my memory, visualizing one person after another, trying to remember what they may have shared as I listened to their problems. I said, "You know, I can't remember if anyone ever shared anything like that with me."

"It may have happened when they were very young and they don't remember it," she answered.

The moment she spoke those words it seemed like a switch clicked in my brain and a picture flashed through my mind of me nearly drowning! It's a miracle I didn't lose control of the car. I could hardly believe it! I said, very haltingly, "Jean, you're not going to believe this."

"Was it you?" she interrupted.

"I'm afraid so," I answered.

To say I was astounded is putting it mildly. I was almost in shock. How could I have forgotten this incident? But I had totally forgotten it until this moment. Now that the memory had surfaced, I gradually began to remember the details.

Living on a farm as a child, I was probably around four or five years old when I went with my brother Raymond (two years older than I) to the river with our closest neighbor and her children. Unknown to my parents, this woman had been drinking heavily. I don't know now whether she was "teasing" me or thought she would try to teach me to swim, but she threw me into the deep water. Every time I struggled to the surface for air, her hand came down on my head and pushed me under.

"If you go under three times, you'll drown." These sage words of some childhood friend (or maybe my brother) came flashing through my mind during those terrifying moments, and I just knew I was drowning! But after what seemed an eternity, and at least three times of going down, someone grabbed me by the hair and pulled me out. I was coughing and sputtering and gasping for air! I cried all the way home, feeling confused and crushed.

And now, seeing this long-forgotten incident as an adult, I could begin to understand the profound effect it had on me. As I relived those memories, I was flooded with the feelings I had experienced at that time, and felt the pain in my heart. I remembered how utterly crushed I had felt — betrayed by the mother of my only playmates! How could she have done that to me? She had tried to kill me! I had felt I was not loved or even worthy to be loved. I had felt ugly and rejected. Surely I deserved to die if she had tried to drown me!

With the release of this memory, I found other memories flooding my thoughts, like a video recording, of incident after incident in my life — things that had happened down through my childhood and early adult years, things that had embarrassed me, and things that had deeply hurt me and caused me to feel worthless and rejected.

My eyes had been opened and I began to understand how I had built a "wall" around my heart to keep others from hurting me. Because deep down in my heart I had felt so inferior, I had put on a mask of superiority — a "false front" to show myself as self-sufficient, competent, mature, and self-assured. Projecting an attitude of being better than others effectively kept people at arm's length!

My mother-in-law had described this very well only a few months earlier when she told me: "You know, Margaret, there have been many times when I wanted to put my arms around you and tell you I love you. But it's like there's been a sign up there saying 'Hands Off! Stay Back! Don't Touch!'"

I had answered her then, "I know, Mom. But God's working on me." And indeed He was! I had no idea, at that point in time, the depth of what He was preparing to do to change my whole life. Already, when we spoke those words on that morning in the summer of 1981, God had been laying the groundwork for me to see some surprising truths about myself.

And by the time Jean Norment came up to see me in January, I had already realized that my <u>motivation</u> had been wrong for all twenty-five years of my church service and Bible study. God had revealed to me over a period of several months through radio messages, Sunday School lessons, pastors' sermons, and personal devotions that I had been diligently working for him, not out of a heart of love and gratitude (as I thought), but in order to earn His approval!

Though I didn't know <u>why</u> that was my motive, I had repented and asked God to help me understand. By this time I had truly come to realize that I could not earn God's approval; I had to accept that I already had it. I could never be worthy of God's love. But He loved me anyway. I was "accepted in the beloved [Jesus]" (Eph. 1:6 KJV). This was now firmly established in my head.

And now, through this "word of knowledge" given by the Holy Spirit through Jean on this January morning, I became aware of this long-buried memory, and the deeply buried hurts and feelings of inferiority were stirred up and exposed to the light. This near-drowning experience had served as the foundation of an emotional wall I had erected over the years to keep out hurts. I was in a prison of my own making!

While this wall kept out hurts, it had also kept me from being able to reach out to others or to receive love from them, or even to know, deep down inside my heart, that God loved me! And so I had been driven to try to prove myself worthy of God's love by doing all the "good works" I could find to do.

Needless to say, at the moment this memory was

unlocked, and all the other memories began to flood my consciousness, I didn't see this whole picture. All I knew at the time was that I was being inundated by memories and my heart was in turmoil. I had no idea how to deal with it all. I found myself trying to pray but I was in such turmoil I didn't even know how to pray!

Although Jean had planned to return to Montgomery, Alabama, the next day without seeing me, she changed her mind when I called and told her what was going on in my soul. "Jean," I said, "I can't get this memory out of my mind! And there are a lot of other memories! I don't know what to do. I don't even know how to pray or <u>what</u> to pray about all this."

"I think I had better come over and talk with you before I leave," she said.

We made arrangements to get her to my house, and I poured out all my emotional turmoil – all the memories and my feelings. By the time I finished, we both realized the truth of her next statement: "I believe we're dealing with a spirit of rejection."

I said "I believe you're right."

Jean led me in some prayers and then prayed for me, and God delivered me from the demonic oppression I had been under all my life, oppression which caused feelings of rejection, fear, condemnation, and I don't know what else. But I know this — God set me free!

In the following days I felt as though I had been under a cloud for years and was now walking in the bright sunshine. For the first time in my life I really knew, deep in my heart, that God loved me. <u>GOD</u> <u>LOVED</u> <u>ME</u>!!!! Hallelujah! What joy filled my soul! My heart was free and open to His love, and songs of praise were on my lips!

There was an immediate radical transformation in me that was readily apparent to all my friends. One of them, Alice Holland, told me a few weeks later that she had told another friend "Something's going on with Margaret!" I'm sure my husband noticed the difference and thought I had gone off the deep end. My youngest son began seeking me out to pray with him at bed-time.

But this was only the beginning of a long-term project God began on that day in January, 1982, to transform my attitudes and outlook, to enable me to love Him and others and to receive their love. God truly did for me what He promised to His chosen people: *"I will give you a new heart and put a new spirit in you; I will remove from you your heart of stone and give you a heart of flesh."* (Ezek. 36:26) I also had to resist the temptation to put the wall back up around my heart, knowing that being able to love others freely and to experience that love from God and them was worth the risk of suffering emotional pain.

My heart was immediately so tender that things hurt it very easily, especially when my husband would ridicule something I said or the things I believed. I learned very quickly how the devil would oppress me in multiple ways if I held on to the least bit of un-forgiveness or anger. Jesus taught that we must forgive in order to <u>be</u> forgiven. But He goes even further, in the parable of the unmerciful servant in Matthew 18:23-35, to show how un-forgiveness opens us up to torment. In <u>verses</u> <u>34-35</u> He says: *"In anger his master turned him over to the jailers to be <u>tortured</u>, until he should pay back all he owed.* **This is how my heavenly Father will treat each of you unless you forgive your brother from your heart**.*"* I learned <u>by experience</u> the necessity of quickly forgiving those who hurt me and of asking God to forgive them and to bless them. This was my path to freedom from torment, and joy in my own heart.

God began a deep cleansing in my heart. Every time I went to church, I would find myself crying almost all the way through the service. I felt like God was scraping out all the awful stuff and doing a thorough cleansing. Each

Sunday I would leave church feeling cleaner and happier than I had ever felt before.

I realized I needed to reprogram my mind by the Word of God to see myself the way <u>God</u> sees me – to know what He says about me as His child. The book of Ephesians was especially helpful in understanding my relationship to God through Jesus, as part of His family. And I began devouring Psalms and Isaiah from the Old Testament, and several books in the New Testament, especially the four Gospels, Ephesians, and Galatians, in order to get to know God better.

Immediately after this experience of deliverance, I somehow knew instinctively that I needed to stop teaching my Bible study group for a while and allow God time to do a greater work in my heart. I waited until I had finished the study of the Gospel of John before I took my sabbatical. I felt God had a call on my life for something big, and I needed to learn how to hear Him speak more clearly to me. During that first year or two after God delivered me, I grew spiritually by leaps and bounds as I learned how to really worship and how to hear God speaking to me.

I've come to realize that each individual is unique and God deals differently with everyone. Some of us "feel" the Spirit moving and others walk totally by faith, without any special feelings. Some of us see visions and others don't. Some hear God speaking very clearly, almost audibly, while others of us get most of our direction from Scripture or inspirations that suddenly come — just a sudden "knowing" inside. Sometimes people may have a vivid dream or simply an inclination to go a certain way.

On one occasion, before I stopped teaching for a season, I was standing at the kitchen sink when I had a sudden revelation from God about Jesus' sufferings. Having only recently discovered for myself the reality of God's love and how sweet it was to have fellowship with Him, as I was meditating on His love I suddenly understood what Jesus was facing when He sweat drops of blood in Gethsemane. I had a sudden "knowing" in my heart of how awful it had been for Jesus, who had known and experienced from all eternity such complete and perfect fellowship with the Father, to be facing the prospects of being separated from God by taking our sin on himself!

I saw very clearly that Jesus, while earnestly praying in such an enormous emotional or spiritual struggle, was not struggling that hard over the coming <u>physical</u> ordeal (although that would be unimaginably painful), but rather was struggling with the prospect of the separation that was about to come between Him and the Father when He would become sin for us! Sin separates us from God. Our sin was about to separate Jesus, for the first time in all eternity, from the Father!

This revelation from God broke my heart. I stood there weeping over what Jesus suffered and the fact that He willingly went through that emotional, spiritual, and physical pain because of His love for us!

Around that same time, when my husband John was out of town again, I visited a non-denominational charismatic church. When he came back, I told him about this new church and persuaded him to visit it too. For one whole year we alternated between this new church and our Baptist church. By the end of that year, John was no longer satisfied in the Baptist church, but neither was he happy with the new one! In fact, he was getting downright miserable. We talked and talked, and prayed and prayed, trying to determine what we should do or what church we could attend.

Somewhere toward the end of this time I was driving over to a fast-food place to get something for dinner when God showed me a very ugly truth about myself. He showed me that, while I was outwardly going through all the motions of submitting to my husband, as He commands wives to do in the Bible, my heart attitude was one of resentment and rebellion. Ooooh! As soon as I saw the truth I repented and asked God to forgive me. I then realized I needed to let go of my own desires and yield completely to my husband, as unto the Lord!

Seeing how miserable he was, and struggling myself with a great desire to be totally in the new church, I had to really buckle down in prayer. One day I was able to fully surrender to God all my desires to attend the new church full time, and I told God I would go wherever He wanted, even if it was to that Baptist church. I asked Him to show John where He wanted us to go. Then I told John that the decision was up to him. I said I wanted him to be happy, and I would go with him wherever he wanted to go. The very next Sunday he told me we would go to the new church. And we never went back to the Baptist church, a denomination we had been in for most of our lives!

One Sunday the church announced a special meeting where they would teach on the Baptism in the Holy Spirit. I asked John if he would like to go, and then waited for several days before mentioning it again. Though John didn't answer right away, he finally did agree to go. I did a lot of praying. At the end of that session the leaders asked everyone who wanted the baptism in the Holy Spirit to pray silently and ask God for this experience. And then they dismissed the meeting.

John didn't tell me whether he had asked for the baptism in the Holy Spirit at the end of that meeting, because he was very reserved when it came to letting me know what was going on with him spiritually. I think he wrongly felt intimidated by my "spirituality." But just a few days later something happened that God permitted me to overhear. I was walking into the bedroom just as John had stepped into the shower. He has a wonderful voice and started to sing a worship song, when it came out in another language! He immediately stopped singing, but I had heard it and rejoiced to myself!

A few days later John burned his hand severely on a soldering iron. As he was pacing up and down outside, I could see his mouth moving and wondered if he was praying. The Holy Spirit began stirring in me that I needed to ask him whether he had received the baptism in the Holy Spirit, since he hadn't volunteered the information.

When I found a chance to ask him, he said "I don't know."

"What do you mean, you don't know?" I asked.

He began to tell me about his experience in the shower (not knowing I had overheard that). Then he said that, while he had been pacing around the yard after burning his hand, he had been doing something strange. He said he didn't know if it was "speaking in tongues" or not, because he could only <u>sing</u> what was coming out of his mouth. And it was a strange sounding chant, almost like an Indian war dance. He sang some for me then, and I have to admit I was puzzled at first. But later, after I had prayed and pondered this for a while, the Lord gave me the answer, and I chuckled. God has a great sense of humor.

You see, John had been inwardly rebelling against this new church because he didn't like the music. They had a very loud band and sang all these modern choruses of Scripture songs, along with what's now called contemporary music. John loved the old hymns. So while he sat in church, he would keep his mouth closed tightly, refusing to sing, even though God had gifted him with a marvelous voice that blesses everyone around him. Is it any wonder that God chose to give him the gift of tongues as a <u>singing</u> language first? I've learned over the years that God will have His way eventually, especially when we say "no" to Him, whether in words or by our actions.

Over the next few years, that new non-denominational church began to take on the appearance of a cult and we thought perhaps we should go to another church. But we were reluctant to leave until we knew for sure where God wanted us to be. We prayed for at least a year while continuing to attend and pray for this church. Finally, when the timing was right, God showed us what He wanted, and we switched to a mainline Pentecostal church, the Assemblies of God (A/G), where we are today.

CHAPTER TWO

Beginnings

A s a young child living on a farm in central Florida, my wildest dream was to move to the Everglades, a possibility Dad was considering at one point. I could never have imagined that one day I would live in another state, much less that I would live in numerous other states and even in several foreign countries for 13 years.

My earliest childhood memory of a religious exposure came from a "revival" being held in a tent at a country crossroad a few miles from our farm. I was probably only five or six years old at the time. I remember Mom and Dad walking forward to shake hands with the preacher during one of the services. I didn't know what they were doing at the time, but later came to realize they were making a public decision to accept Christ as their Savior. I remember standing on the banks of a river shortly afterwards on a Sunday afternoon watching them and others being baptized. It was a wonderful experience for me as the congregation sang, "Shall We Gather At the River?"

The immediate difference this made in my life was that Dad quit drinking, and for the first time we began attending the little Baptist church in the community of Welcome, Florida, about five or six miles from our farm. I say "community," but all that was there were a few homes spaced at good distances, this very small country church, and a grocery store with a gas pump and a kerosene pump. This was the source of fuel for the farmers to light their homes when the power was out, cook their food and heat their homes, and, of course, run their trucks so they could farm and market their crops. This store was also the place to buy food supplies, get tobacco products and "chew the fat" (that's what they called what we might call gossip) with each other. The store also had a crank-up telephone they could use if they had an emergency or a need to get hold of the doctor, because only one or two of them had their own telephone service.

My playmates were my brother Raymond and the little boys across the road, or whatever children happened to be living in our tenant house nearby. I was a tomboy, always climbing trees, shooting marbles, playing with slingshots and knives, or occasionally going hunting with a .22 rifle, as well as doing all sorts of other typical boys' rough and tumble stuff.

Of course, I also had to help Mom and Dad, along with my brothers and sisters (I was the youngest of seven children), with the work of the farm. We grew all sorts of crops at one time or another, a vast variety of different vegetables and/or fruit. We had to prepare beds and plant seeds or seedlings, hoe weeds, irrigate the crops, do whatever was necessary to save them from frost or freezing in the winter time, and harvest the crops when they were ready.

One of the biggest joys of my life came on those few occasions when Dad would let me go with him and Raymond to the farmers' market in Tampa late at night to sell whatever produce we had just harvested. There was such an excitement about walking in those late-night-to-predawn hours of the morning through the area where all the various vegetables and fruits were on display for the grocery store buyers. On many occasions Dad would buy a basket of bananas or mangoes or something else to provide us with a rare treat. Often we wouldn't get home until shortly after sunrise, sometimes just in time for Dad to drop us off at school.

It was during one such trip that I purchased some cigarettes from a vending machine and began my experiment with smoking. I got away with it for two or three months until Dad caught me. The tongue-lashing he gave me was worse than any spanking could have been, scarring my soul with the harshness of his words. But I've never smoked since then. Only once in my adult life was I seriously tempted to try smoking again, but God helped me to resist.

My father was a very harsh disciplinarian in dealing with my youngest brother and my sisters. Our oldest brother Lee was away in the Air Force and then college as I went through my early years, so I didn't get to know him very well. But my brother Raymond was always getting whipped and yelled at by Dad. As I watched, I resolved not to do the things that brought him punishment. In other words, I learned to behave in the best way I could so I wouldn't get whipped. On one occasion I did receive a serious beating with a belt because I tried to rescue my sister whom Dad was chasing around the house. I was afraid he was going to kill her. The physical pain and large whelps that resulted from his belt on my back were small compared to the emotional pain caused by that beating.

Many years later I came to realize that my fear of punishment from my earthly father had shaped my feelings about God as a big policeman in the sky watching for us to do wrong so He could punish us. While I grew up doing the best I knew how in order to please Dad and avoid his anger, I was also learning to do my best in order to please God and avoid His wrath.

When I was about nine or ten years of age, the Welcome Baptist Church had a revival that I well remember. One particular sermon got my attention. The evangelist was preaching a vivid message about hell, and when the invitation to accept Christ came, I began to shake all over. I had a deep conviction in my heart that I was on my way to hell and that I needed to give my heart to Jesus to escape that terrible place. I thought it was necessary to walk up front and take the preacher's hand just like my parents had done. But I was very scared. I held on to the pew with all my strength, which wasn't much because I was shaking so badly.

Since my dad was very critical and judgmental, I was afraid he would ask me all sorts of questions about it if I did such a thing. And because I was afraid I wouldn't know what to answer him, I let that fear keep me glued to the spot where I stood. After what seemed like an eternity, the song accompanying the invitation stopped and I managed to escape, but I couldn't get away from the feeling that I really needed to give my heart to Jesus. While I didn't understand at the time what was going on, I came to realize much later that God's Holy Spirit was moving on my heart and convicting me of my sin and of my need to receive Jesus as my Savior. But I was steadfastly resisting that effort as it happened again Sunday after Sunday.

Dad gave up his losing struggle to make a living on our farm in central Florida when I was ten years old. He managed to sell our 120 acres of land with two houses on it for $8500! That was barely enough to pay off his debts and move us into a small house-trailer in a place called New Ellenton, South Carolina. Dad had gotten a job there as a pipe-fitter, helping to build the Savannah River Project, a facility for making hydrogen bombs. How exciting it was for my brother and me when we actually moved out of the state of Florida! I would never have dreamed that I would ever leave Florida, let alone move to South Carolina!

At this time we began attending a fairly large Baptist church in this little town. But I seldom felt God's Spirit moving on my heart then. I had hardened my heart in my efforts to resist the pull of the Holy Spirit, until I began to get fearful that maybe I had hardened it too far and could no longer accept Jesus. I sometimes felt like I was standing on a cliff and a rescue rope was swinging toward me and then away from me, like a pendulum — but it was swinging in a smaller and smaller arc, getting further and further away, seldom swinging near me any more.

One day Mom told me my brother Raymond was going to join the church. He apparently thought he was supposed to become a preacher. I remember thinking I couldn't let him do that and leave me behind! I started asking God, that if it wasn't too late, would He please move on my heart again, and I would accept Jesus. When Raymond went forward to take the preacher's hand, I began to get that "feeling" again. It was a feeling of being very scared. Shaking all over and with my heart pounding, I was still fearful and struggling with whether to go forward or not. I finally decided I couldn't let my brother become a Christian without me. So I took courage and went up front too. The preacher led me in a prayer to receive Jesus as my Savior and I entered into a brand new life. Raymond and I were baptized together.

I didn't realize it at that time, but found out much later that I could have opened my heart and asked Jesus to come in all by myself without going forward to talk to the preacher. But I also knew the Bible says it's important to tell others that Jesus is your Savior and Lord, and to obey Jesus' commands, and to follow His example of being baptized.

From that point on, I was at the church every time they had something going on. Even business meetings fascinated me! It was all so exciting! I began reading the Bible and studying as hard as I could so I could be the very best Christian possible. I took every study course, seminary correspondence course, or whatever else was available over the years, in order to learn everything I could about the Bible. I was determined to prove myself worthy of God's love and forgiveness. Without realizing it, I was entering into a life of bondage to "works"— gradually becoming more and more legalistic as time went by.

We lived in New Ellenton for only three and a half years. Then my father became an itinerant worker, moving us whenever and wherever he could find a job. We spent anywhere from three months to a year in several different locations. One of the places where we lived for one year was Douglasville, Georgia. I experienced another breakthrough in my spiritual journey in a little church on a dirt road across the railroad tracks from the farm on which we had our trailer parked. At the end of one of the services, as the preacher gave the call for people to come to the altar and make a decision for Christ, I suddenly felt another "conviction" coming over me. I had a strong impression that God wanted me to be a missionary. Again, as I had in the little church in Welcome, Florida, I stood rooted to the spot, clinging to the pew in front of me, my heart pounding like it was coming out of my chest. I've never seen an altar call go on for so long. We sang and sang and sang. The song we were singing had six or eight verses and we sang every one of them at least twice! The preacher was waiting for someone to respond, but I don't know whether he knew he was waiting for me. I was resisting the Holy Spirit's call. Finally I gathered my courage and went down to the altar to give my life for missions.

After that I began to correspond with the foreign mission board of the Southern Baptist Convention, learning what I needed to do to prepare to become a missionary. My heart was sold out to serve God, whatever that meant.

My dad's job in that area didn't last long so we moved our trailer down to Orlando, Florida, while Dad looked for work. I don't know what work he did that summer, but the time came in the fall to move again. I guess he found a job in Alabama, because we spent the next year in Childersburg, not far from Birmingham. My brother and I had great adventures there. There was an undeveloped natural cavern outside of town that was rumored to be part of a series of caverns stretching all the way to Talladega, many miles away. This cave was used by the soldiers during the Civil War. We heard, also, that the huge cavern in the front, with a flat floor, had been used for dances in the previous century until the music caused pieces of the stalactites to break off and fall. That could be deadly! Raymond and some friends decided to explore those caves. I was very frightened that he would get lost.

I loved the mountains and the hills. And for the first time in my life I got to see some snow that winter. My church there paid my way to attend the Foreign Missions Conference at the Southern Baptist's conference center called Ridgecrest, near Asheville, North Carolina. I had never ridden on a commercial bus, so I was in awe and thrilled beyond measure to travel on a Greyhound bus through those wonderful Blue Ridge Mountains to the conference center all by myself! The thrill of rubbing elbows with foreign missionaries and new missionary appointees while there was almost more than I could stand! One particular newly appointed missionary who deeply impressed me was a woman physician who had been appointed to Egypt. I spent several hours over those days talking one-on-one with her. I even corresponded with her for several years.

While in Childersburg, I also had the unique opportunity of becoming the author of a religious column for a weekly newspaper that was started during the time I lived there.

What a thrill for me, as a sophomore in high school, to have a newspaper column! After only one year in this magical place, we returned to Orlando, Florida, where I finished my final two years of high school.

We lived in a trailer park on a lake. I remember sitting on the dock, feeding the little minnows and fish with bread and catching small fish on a hook using balls of dough made by squeezing bread. I would either throw the minnows back or cut them up to use for bait trying to catch larger fish. A few times we were invited out on the lake in someone's boat. We couldn't go swimming in the lake because alligators were an ever-present danger. But it was a fun time.

While living there I met and dated John for probably a year and a half. We were married just a few days shy of my high school graduation. What a shock for my English teacher when I introduced her to my husband at the graduation ceremonies! For years afterwards I felt guilty about that, remembering the shocked look on her face. I knew she had held high hopes for me, as I was one of her best students. I guess I had disappointed her greatly. But my parents didn't have the money to send me to college, I knew nothing about scholarships or loans for college, and John wanted to get married sooner, rather than later. We thought we might be able to put each other through school to become missionaries.

John was in the Air Force when we met, stationed at McCoy Air Force Base. After we married and I graduated from high school, I became an information operator for the telephone company. In a few months time, John was suddenly and unexpectedly discharged (honorably) from the Air Force and out looking for work. On the very same day, a deacon in our church "just happened" to be looking for a new employee for his plumbing/air-conditioning company, and God brought the two of them together at the church prayer meeting that night. I have learned over the years that there are no coincidences in the lives of God's children. But He works behind the scenes to orchestrate and prepare the way for us in life.

Shortly after John started working for this new company, I became its receptionist/ PBX operator. A PBX was a telephone exchange which enabled me, wearing headphones, to answer calls and plug them into the proper jack to connect them to the appropriate office. We hoped to save our money toward college. But I didn't count on an unexpected pregnancy within that first year of marriage.

Two weeks after the birth of our first son, John Mark, we moved from Orlando to the panhandle of Florida's gulf coast. John's mother and stepfather (who prided himself on being an atheist) owned a foreign car sales and service company in Fort Walton Beach and had asked John to come to work for them. They promised John that they would start him out at the same pay he had been making in the plumbing/air-conditioning company. We had expectations that things would get better, and we would be closer to our dream of going to college. But this move was a major mistake, which we could have avoided had we known how to hear more clearly from God and given ourselves to more prayer about it or sought advice from mature friends or counselors before we made the decision.

John's stepfather Bill hated me and made it abundantly clear that he thought John had married beneath him and that it was my fault John didn't go to college. Bill was an atheist and we clashed on many occasions. He seriously took advantage of John, requiring him to work extremely long days, opening the business in the early hours of the morning, and closing it late at night.

And then he cut John's salary in half. Many years later, I came to believe (whether rightly or wrongly, I don't really know) that he cut John's pay hoping I would leave John if the going got tough enough. We could not have survived if John's mother had not brought us groceries from time to time.

Eventually, John acquired a job with Douglas Aircraft Company, which was testing an air-launched ballistic missile at Eglin Air Force Base nearby. Thinking things were going to be okay, we decided to have another baby and Robert Kenneth was born. But by the time Bobby was six months old, the missile program was dropped by the government and everyone was laid off. Fortunately, Douglas Aircraft offered John a job out in California, near Sacramento, but on the condition that he move himself there. So we sold our house trailer, built a two-wheeled cargo-hauling trailer, and packed our belongings for a long drive! That was truly an adventure for me as we drove through snow-covered mountains and deserts.

When we first moved there, we realized it would be much more expensive than any place we had lived before. Not seeing how we would be able to afford it, we decided maybe we shouldn't continue to tithe until we could see how far John's salary would stretch. But we were suddenly besieged by all sorts of unexpected expenses, including a broken collar bone in our oldest little boy! We immediately realized that when we stopped being obedient to God we had moved out from under His umbrella of protection. We saw that we could ill afford to withhold God's tithe, and chose to trust Him to meet our needs. We have never stopped tithing since then, and God has always faithfully provided for us.

For six months we lived in a furnished duplex apartment in Rancho Cordova, California. Then an opportunity opened up for John to work on Johnston Island, in the Pacific, for nine months, helping test missiles there. He would be receiving lots of extra pay, which would help us get on our feet financially. We hoped he could be transferred to Orlando after his time on the island.

Since families could not go to Johnston Island, I took the two boys and moved back to Orlando, to be near my parents. They were living in a trailer in a little suburb called Casselberry, north of Orlando, and I had to rent a house for me and the kids. I'll never forget sitting in that little house with the boys and hearing the overwhelming news of President John F. Kennedy's assassination! How I wished John was with me! He called me that day when he also heard this terrible news. He was able to come home for Christmas, and then went back again.

When John's tours on Johnston Island ended, he wasn't able to get transferred to Orlando. So I drove back to California alone with our two very young boys. We moved into a duplex apartment again, until we managed to buy a house that had been repossessed by the government. We were able to close on this house with no down payment and to purchase a minimum amount of furniture — just enough to get by. That began a wonderful period in our life when we did a lot of sight-seeing, camping, fishing, and serving the Lord in our local church.

We thoroughly enjoyed living in a location where any kind of scenery or entertainment imaginable was available within a few hours' drive (or a day at most). During the summers we would be off nearly every Saturday and at least one weekend per month, going camping in the wonderful State and National parks, exploring, and playing in the snow on the higher elevations. We had Lassen Volcanic National Park, with a live volcano, within a four or five hours' drive. Crater Lake, in Oregon, was only a few hours further. The location of Sutter's Mill, where the famous Gold Rush began, was only an hour away. We took in many other fascinating sights: Calaveras Big Trees State Park where the huge Sequoia and Redwood trees grow; Yosemite National Park; Disneyland and Marine World; Hearst Castle at San Luis Obispo; Reno and Carson City, Nevada (where the silver mine was located); San Francisco's Golden Gate Bridge and cable cars with the Embarcadero; and Lake

Tahoe. In the winter it was only a couple of hours to the deep snow for tobogganing.

We loved our time in California and lived there for at least seven years. John was contentedly working his way up to a supervisory position in the calibration lab with Douglas Aircraft Company, where he had started at a position lower than that of a technician. He worked at this company's facilities just outside Sacramento, near the town of Rancho Cordova. These facilities at that time were being used to test the 4th stage of the Saturn moon rocket which would ultimately be used to send our astronauts out of earth's orbit to the moon.

CHAPTER THREE

God's Plan Unfolds

In the mid 60's, in California, we were both heavily involved in our Baptist church, John as a deacon, and I as a Sunday School teacher of married young people. On Sunday evenings we both worked with children aged nine through twelve in Training Union. Training Union was a program intended to train children and adults in how to be teachers and leaders. The participants would learn by doing. I worked with the Women's Missionary Union as well. I continued to pursue my writing interests, and had the privilege of having several articles published at various times in our statewide Baptist paper. This was another "thrill of a lifetime," and I thank God for it.

We were very happy at this church with a wonderful pastor who was everything you could ever want in a pastor. In all the years we have been attending various churches, we have never had another pastor who really seemed to care so much about us. It was in this church where our two young sons opened their hearts to Jesus. Bobby was only six years of age when he started expressing a desire to accept Jesus as his Savior. Because he was so young, I wanted to be very sure he knew what he was doing. So I took him to see our pastor, who talked with him and led him in a prayer to receive God's forgiveness through Jesus Christ.

During our years in this church, California Baptists had a statewide evangelistic thrust called "Encounter." Every church participating received specialized training in evangelism. We learned how to give our full testimony in a meaningful way in one minute. This was in order to go to every home in the state, and give the resident our personal one-minute testimony along with a special edition of the Gospel of John which contained testimonies of V.I.P.'s who loved the Lord. Included with the special Gospel of John was an invitation to attend a huge crusade that would be held in a stadium following our door-to-door outreach.

I was asked to be in charge of this evangelistic thrust in our church, which meant I would organize and train our people, divide up our assigned territory on the map, and make assignments to the volunteers to cover the door-to-door event. This was invaluable training for me that I would be able to use throughout my life in sharing my own testimony as well as teaching others evangelism. On the day of the stadium crusade I served as a prayer counselor to minister to people who responded to the invitation to accept Christ.

One day, after we had been in California for about five years, my husband bought a magazine on the spur of the moment, a magazine he never had read before. Something must have caught his attention on the cover. Inside he found a small classified ad (about one column inch in size) seeking people who would like to work for the U.S. Government overseas. It intrigued John because when he had first met me, nearly a decade earlier, I was already preparing to become a foreign missionary. Before we got married, he had come to believe that God was also calling him to that ministry. But somehow those dreams had been dampened over time, and put aside as just another impossible dream.

After seeing the ad and discussing it with me, and mostly out of curiosity, he followed the instructions in the ad and sent off the required information to start an application process that would ultimately take two years to complete. Not having any information on exactly what this employment involved, he was really just trying to explore the possibility, reserving any decisions until he could see whether it would be something we wanted to do.

A couple of weeks went by and John received a phone call from Washington, D.C., from someone saying he was coming out to Palo Alto, CA, about two weeks later and was interested in interviewing him. John agreed to meet him at an arranged time and place to see what the job was all about. When John returned from the meeting, he said his first impression was negative. He didn't think he would be interested in the job, because it would require him to be away from his family a large part of the time. John has always been very much a family man, wanting to be with his wife and children and not be traveling around all alone to different countries. He told me he had told the interviewer how stupid the test he had taken was. He didn't realize at the time (though he would find out years later) that the man interviewing him had himself written that test!

Yet John didn't feel he should close the door, so he allowed the application process to continue, to see what would come of it. The next step was to fill out lengthy forms for a security clearance and to take our entire family to the nearby Air Force base's medical facilities for thorough physicals to see if we were physically and psychologically good candidates to endure the unique conditions and stress of living overseas and doing this type of work.

This process itself took several months, and finally we received a letter saying they had finished all the necessary clearances and they felt he was a qualified candidate. However, they said they had no openings at that time but would keep his application on file. We took that as a brush-off and figured we would never hear from them again. So we had to get on with our lives.

Then my mother, who still lived in central Florida, was diagnosed with colon cancer and given only six weeks to two or three months to live. I was heartbroken. Some older friends from our church volunteered to take care of our two young boys to enable me to go back home for a week's visit while Mom was still alive. I flew home to see her and returned with a very heavy heart, knowing I would never see her again on this earth. After much intense prayer she rallied and lived another six or eight months! We thought God had healed her.

Meanwhile, our neighborhood began deteriorating. Our next-door neighbor sold her house to a family with several children who moved in and brought another family in with them. The "good-neighbor" fence between our yards got pulled over. We repaired the fence and put a lock on our gate, only to find the kids next door climbing the fence when we would leave home and playing with the toys in our back yard. We began to see our children's toys disappear or get mysteriously broken.

Like a "good Christian," I knew I was supposed to love my neighbors, but they were really making it difficult!

Also about this time, our church abruptly changed pastors, and the man who came to serve in that capacity was really not a pastor but an evangelist. He was a wonderful speaker, but had no administrative skills. He also seemed to be severely lacking in common sense when it came to dealing with people. From the beginning, he began doing things that we felt were unethical, and some of the advertising stunts he pulled were even dangerous.

Because he was a powerful evangelistic preacher, people were flocking to our church. But after a few months, they would leave again because of the things they saw going on.

My husband, as one of the leaders of the church, felt he should say something to the pastor. That got us immediately on his black list and totally out of favor. We prayed about whether we should leave and find another church, but we were very much aware of our influence and didn't want to cause even more people to leave. So we stayed and prayed.

My husband began seeing the handwriting on the wall concerning his job since the moon rocket program was approaching its end. Knowing that other companies in the aerospace industry were already laying off thousands of workers at that time, and knowing he had very little formal education to qualify him for another job with another company in that field, he felt he had no likely prospect of getting a job when the work was finished and he was laid off.

Then, another "bad" family moved into the circle across the street from us and began throwing wild parties. People would be sitting in their cars right at the curb in front of our house until all hours of the morning, keeping us awake by arguing, talking, laughing, playing their radios at high volume, and throwing beer and whiskey bottles and cans into our yard. We finally reached a point where we decided we had to sell our house and move. We also thought it was a good idea to cut our ties in preparation for going to another city to get work, if that became necessary.

Knowing that the housing market was glutted by people who had already lost their jobs, we decided to try to find someone to take over the payments on our house, so we could move out. After much prayer, we put the ad in a small community weekly paper with very limited circulation. We received a few calls, and the first person who called for information actually came to see the house and decided to buy it! So we thanked God, made the deal, and set a closing date six weeks away.

Then came the crunch! While there were many houses for sale, there were hardly any for rent. I was really in a squeeze as I looked and looked and couldn't find a suitable house in an area we liked at a price we could afford. I found one house we liked in a nice area, but it was in terrible condition inside. I have never in all my life seen a house so filthy. The previous tenants had continually used the fireplace with a faulty flue, and the entire house was coated with soot. They also had several dogs living in the house and the once light yellow carpet was darkly stained and smelled of urine and feces. The yellow drapes were black with dust and soot and also rotten. The bathroom cabinets had been left full of unmentionable filth. The kitchen had a thick layer of grease and grime on counters, cabinets, walls, and ceiling. The real estate agent had lost track of the owner and thus couldn't get the necessary permission to spend money to clean and refurbish the house. Consequently, the realtor had been unable to rent it to anyone.

I was so desperate, I made a deal with the agent. If the agency would knock off half the first month's rent and provide the paint, I would clean up the house for them. They accepted the offer gladly. The work I would have to do would later prove to be a blessing for me ordained of God.

Finally, also we bit the bullet and decided to move to a new church. About a week or two after we started attending the new church, and the week before we were to start moving into this nasty rental house, my mother died. I flew back to Florida for the funeral, came back home on Thursday, and we began to move our belongings on Friday. With moving and then cleaning and painting of our "new" home, I would have a lot of busy work to keep my mind occupied so I wouldn't dwell so much on losing my mom.

The very weekend that we were moving, the people at the State Department in Washington tried to call us! Our phones were useless because we weren't there to answer them and the new house wasn't yet connected, and we had no answering machine. (I don't know whether they even existed then!) When they finally reached John at work on Monday, they offered him a job in the Foreign Service, saying their immediate opening was not overseas, but in Washington, D.C.!

This seemed to be a wonderful move, putting me closer to my family, which would help in my grieving process over Mom's death. But there was a big hitch! It seems the government didn't have the funds to move us to Washington. We had to pay for our own move, and then they would hire John!

We didn't have the money to move ourselves there. We had no savings. John had barely made enough for our growing family to live on. But we had invested a tiny portion of his paycheck in the company's stock over a long period. We had nine shares, which had doubled to eighteen just a few months before, when Douglas Aircraft Company merged with another company and became McDonnell-Douglas.

As we looked at the situation, we could see God's hand in this as we had never seen it before. What timing! When we first sent in the response to the ad, our lives were happy and fulfilled, and we had no desire to move. And when John had gone to the interview, he had no desire for this particular job. But in the two years since he had answered that ad, every facet of our lives had changed. God had allowed the State Department to wait before offering John a job, until all the things in our life — our home, our church, and John's work situation — had come to a point where we were willing and free to move!

Yet how could we pay for a move to Washington? The eighteen shares of stock were all we had in terms of available financial assets. We got estimates from the moving company on their costs; considered what it would take to put down deposits on an apartment and utilities in the Washington area; then added costs for food, motels and gas for our own trip to Washington. We found that we needed at least $900 to move. (This was in 1968!) We figured we would have to sell the stock for $50 per share in order to have what we needed to make this move. But for many years this stock had been very stable, fluctuating between $40 and $42 dollars a share on the stock market.

Feeling very sure, because of the awesome timing and circumstances, that this was God's plan for us, but wanting to be absolutely certain, we put out a "fleece." We asked God to cause the price of this stock to go up to $50 a share if He wanted John to take this job that He seemed to be opening up. We told a stockbroker friend of ours we wanted him to sell the stock if it climbed to $50 a share. Within a few days the stock leaped to $52 per share, and the broker sold it for $50 each! Immediately after that, the shares of stock in this company plummeted into the $20's and stayed in that range for many years afterward!

We had our answer and the money we needed, so we began making plans to move. We knew with a greater certainty than we had ever had before that this was God's will for us at this time.

However, I had signed a rental lease with the real estate agent. Again we had to seek God's help to give us favor. I had been working very hard, scrubbing, washing, and painting. Someone suggested that adding a little vinegar to the water with which I shampooed the carpet would help eliminate the stench of urine. I had to shampoo it several times to get most of the stains and smell out of the carpet. I washed the drapes, and patched them where they were torn during the washing. I painted the bathrooms and scrubbed the kitchen. When I talked to the real estate people, they inspected the house and began bringing people to look at it even before I finished all the work, and they had it leased by the time we were ready to move! Not only that, but they refunded all my deposit!

You might think surely we were solid in our faith that this was all God's plan and purpose, and that everything was going to work out just fine. Well that's exactly the way I felt about it. However, I didn't realize that John was fraught with anxiety over quitting his job. He was also trading a better paying job for only a <u>promise</u> of more job security and benefits. He was especially worried about moving his family to Washington with no job guarantee in hand. (I didn't realize it then but this was a very valid concern, as we learned a few years later when we saw the State Department promise other people the same deal and then renege on it after they had gone to the expense of moving themselves to Washington!)

The weather at this time of year was also a factor bringing much concern. Our move was in December, and we were taking the most direct route between Sacramento and Washington. This route took us across the northern part of America, including Salt Lake City, Chicago, and Pittsburgh. After we headed out, we found ourselves one day ahead of a blizzard coming across the country!

Both of us were also worried about the condition of our car and whether it would be able to make such a trip. It was several years old, and we had begun to sense that something bad was about to happen. In the middle of Nebraska, where the flat open prairie was wide and empty, and towns were small and a hundred miles apart, we came through a town that had a total of three traffic lights. At the first traffic light our car began to show signs of major trouble. It was making a terrible noise and was very sluggish, not wanting to move at all. We turned around at the last light and found a dealer for our car. We were surprised to find they had a transmission specialist. Not only that, but he wasn't very busy. It took less than two hours for him to make the repairs, which we just knew were going to be very costly. Imagine our surprise to find it cost only $12.50!

When the mechanic told us what the problem was and said "I don't know how you were able to move at all," we looked at each other and said, "We do." We went on our way rejoicing in a deeper assurance of God's protection and provision, knowing more than ever that we were right in the center of His will. This was the assurance John needed to get rid of the butterflies of uncertainty about our future, and he continued then with the same conviction that I already had that God was watching over us and that this was indeed His will for us after all.

CHAPTER FOUR

A Road to Change

While I was only a teenager, I had begun teaching children in Vacation Bible School. After I met and married John, I graduated to teaching young singles, and then young married couples in our church Sunday School. Then some years later I was asked to teach adults who were older than I. As my husband and I ultimately moved around the world, I would teach neighborhood Bible studies or Sunday School classes for women or couples, including missionaries, in our church. All these things were part of the "works" I ended up doing, thinking I was doing them because I loved God, only to discover much later that I was actually trying to earn God's approval.

At the time of the birth of our first son, we gave him the good Biblical name John Mark, intending to call him by his middle name. We dedicated him to the Lord at the age of two weeks. I just knew he would grow up to be a preacher! I determined I would "raise him right"; I would do everything in my power to be sure he learned to obey me and God!

What I didn't know was that this little boy had a mind of his own. If you've ever heard of the "willful," or strong-willed, child, then you have an idea what I went through with him. Mark and I fought down through the years, with my heart becoming more and more hardened, demanding obedience at the expense of love and mercy. It was a fight of the wills to see who would win on any issue. Without realizing it, I was behaving toward Mark the same way my dad had behaved toward my brother. I was constantly spanking him and screaming at him.

I didn't know the importance of demonstrating my love and showing him affection. In my ignorance, I was afraid a hug would undo the spanking. Is it any wonder he grew up hating me and rebelling against God? Of course, I've since learned how very important it is for our children to know that we love them, especially when we've had to discipline them!

Our second son Bobby was a perfect "angel," until his older brother's behavior began corrupting his. He learned to be manipulative and deceptive. These two brothers were like the Biblical Jacob and Esau in behavior, as well as in their parents' reactions to them. Bobby was a quiet, shy, creative, intellectual type who was clumsy with his hands. Mark was outgoing, hated school work, and loved doing things with his hands. Bobby had a sincere heart for the things of God, and Mark appeared to have little use for them. Bobby was my favorite and Mark was John's. This led to many problems over the years.

I thank and praise God that He has since corrected all our mistakes, though it took many years of prayerful waiting upon the Lord, and was accompanied by much heartbreak. God has brought about reconciliation between Mark and me, which I will tell about later, and He caused John and Bobby to establish a wonderful father-son relationship for a few years before Bobby's untimely death in October, 1998.

When John took the job with the U. S. Department of State, in December, 1968, his immediate assignment was in

Washington, D.C. This was the best of all possible arrangements for many reasons.

First, it took us from the west coast to the east coast, within easier driving distance to my family, at a time when I was heartbroken over my mother's death. Also at that time my dad was delving into occult activities which would ultimately result in his involuntary commitment to a mental ward at the hospital and later in a group home under heavy sedation for over twenty years until his death. Because of this I did a lot of in-depth study of the occult and the dire consequences for Christians who get involved in such activities. Many years later, this led me to an over-emphasis on demons, attributing far too much power to them, as many Christians do today. But God eventually brought me to a healthy balance.

Second, it gave John an opportunity to see whether or not he would really like this job before we were committed to living overseas. It was sort of a "breaking in" time for all of us. It was shortly after he began his new career that he discovered that the author of the test he had called stupid when he was first being interviewed was none other than the interviewer! In fact, this man was John's first supervisor! That added to our sense of wonder at how God had opened this door anyway, two years after the application process had begun! I found myself once again teaching an older women's class in Sunday School in our church in northern Virginia.

After nearly two years in the Washington area, living in Alexandria, Virginia, we were unable to make ends meet financially. John's pay was not stretching nearly far enough, and I was desperately searching for a part-time job. Potential employers didn't want to hire me, knowing that I could be shipped overseas in a few months. The fact that I had been out of the job market for almost ten years and had very little working experience before that, didn't help my prospects either.

Through God's grace we were soon shipped to our first assignment in Panama City, Republic of Panama, in the spring of 1970. I say "shipped" because we chose to travel to our new home, with our car in the hold, on a passenger ship belonging to the well-known Grace Lines. Unfortunately, this ship turned out to be a glorified "banana boat"— a rusting freighter doubling as a cruise ship.

Being seasick was no fun, but still we found this journey to be a wonderful experience, providing many thrills for us all. One of the intriguing things for me about this time on the ship was to stand at the rail, watching the schools of flying fish going from wave to wave in the air! It was a simple pleasure, but one which could occupy me for hours. Of course there were many other activities, including shuffleboard, checkers, walking the decks, movies, and swimming. Our boys enjoyed the latter activity, even though the pool was rusty and extremely small.

We stopped off for sight-seeing in Bermuda and the Dominican Republic on our way, and again in Colon at the Caribbean end of the Panama Canal. We were awed at the engineering marvel of the canal and its locks, and thoroughly enjoyed crossing the Isthmus of Panama on a ship! And then we disembarked in Balboa on the Pacific Ocean to begin our new posting.

We loved Panama City once we got settled. It was tropical, it was exciting, and it was a wonderful first assignment. Many of the people there spoke English so it wasn't too difficult to communicate. It was an easier transition to be half-in and half-out of a foreign environment. We were barely in a foreign country, being only a few miles outside the American territory of the Panama Canal Zone. And because we were diplomats, we were able to partake of American shopping by way of all the U.S. military exchanges and an American-styled commissary run by the Panama Canal Company. We were eligible to be treated by the doctors in clinics at the American hospital in the Canal Zone, if we wished. But there were times when I preferred going to a doctor in Panama City.

Our apartment building was built above the home of the owner. Each floor was a single apartment, accessible by the outdoor stairs or elevator. We lived on the fifth floor, actually six floors above the ground, with a balcony overlooking a small airport on the Punta Paitilla in the Pacific Ocean. This provided hours of reflection as I watched the beautiful scenery, airplanes taking off and landing, and the fascinating life around me. There's no way to describe the beauty of the sunset as the sun descended over the ocean past the airport. I don't believe I've ever seen more gorgeous sunsets.

The apartment was very open, with a portion of it completely exposed to the outside where clothes lines hung to enable the clothes to dry in a climate where rain was frequent and extremely heavy. That same openness provided access to a cat-burglar on two separate occasions, even on the sixth floor! I was about eight months pregnant when one of the burglars came into my bedroom and stole my purse from right beside my bed! John was away on a trip to another country at the time. Thankfully, I didn't have a lot of money in it at that particular time (though I usually carried large quantities). Apparently he was only after the cash, since he left the rest of my purse's contents, including all my credit cards and identification, on the stair landing outside the front door.

On another occasion, we were rudely awakened by the Panamanian police pounding on the door, wanting to come in to search for a burglar who had been seen climbing from balcony to balcony up the outside of our building. We were very happy to have them search under all the beds and in every closet, especially when we discovered that he had already removed several panes of glass from the jalousie windows and bent the screen in the process of trying to break into our living room from our balcony! I'm sure he was on the balcony at the very moment the police pounded on our door, and he fled immediately. Praise God for watching over us!

Many of the people living around us were also Americans who were lower ranking military personnel and could not get into quarters in the Canal Zone. I conducted a Bible study in the apartment of one such family. Several young American women attended this study, and I had the privilege of leading one of them to accept Jesus as her Savior when I went to visit her during the time I taught that class.

Our sons were actively involved in Boy Scouts through our church in the Canal Zone, and my husband even became an assistant scout leader. It was good for John to be working alongside our boys in this program. It helped make up for the fact he was away from home on trips to other countries quite a bit of the time.

Several events of our stay in Panama will remain forever seared in my memory. One was the night we awoke to our bed shaking and all the jalousie windows rattling furiously. At first I wondered why John was shaking our bed. Then I realized we were having an earthquake! I jumped out of bed and ran to the window. Looking down on the street, I could see people below running into the streets outside their homes. I thought surely our apartment building was going to collapse and we would ride it down from our sixth floor perch, praying we wouldn't get buried. But the quake was of short duration, although it seemed like an eternity. The epicenter was a little way out in the Pacific Ocean, and damage was not as bad as it could have been had the quake lasted longer. It registered 6.5 on the Richter scale.

Another unexpected event was my coming down with mononucleosis and then learning I had also become pregnant with our third child, at a time when our other boys were nine and eleven! It was a very difficult time for me, emotionally and physically, to carry this child to full term. First of all, I was very concerned that the mononucleosis virus could have damaged my baby. Everything I could find in medical literature indicated there was a possibility, although the doctor lied to me in order to try to put my fears to rest. And secondly, to be pregnant was extremely hard in a tropical climate when my strength was so drained by this illness. There were times when I wondered whether I would make it. Going up one flight of stairs would so exhaust me that I would have to stop and rest for a few minutes before I could even go on about my business.

One time when I was about seven or eight months pregnant I returned from a grocery shopping trip to find the power out in my building. I couldn't use the intercom to get the maid to come down and get the groceries. I had frozen foods that needed to be taken up right away in order to put them in the freezer. I thought I would die trying to climb all those flights of stairs to get to our apartment, six floors above the ground.

People in the great country of America take their utilities for granted except for when a storm knocks out power for a brief period. But people in other countries often lose their power for hours or days at a time (if they even have it to begin with), and other utilities as well. All of my years overseas have made me very grateful for the blessings America enjoys.

Somewhere within the last few weeks of pregnancy things got really difficult between me and our oldest son John Mark. He was eleven years old at the time and almost out of control in his behavior. He and I got into a showdown that turned into a literal fistfight that scared our maid half out of her wits. Mark was pummeling me with his fists!

John was out of the country on one of his work trips at the time, and I was still so upset when he returned that I gave him an ultimatum. It was Mark or me. I could no longer live with our oldest son, and I actually wanted my husband to choose between Mark and me! My emotions were no doubt strongly influenced by the hormones raging in my body at the time. But I am not making excuses for myself. I am utterly ashamed today of how I behaved. But that was the reality of my life at that moment in time.

Fortunately, I have a wonderful husband who is always patient and hard to ruffle. He was able to bring me back to my senses so I could see how utterly impossible my demands were. When God finally showed me my heart, many years later, and how big my mistakes were, Mark was already on his own and had developed what seemed an impossible wall of anger and resentment toward me around his heart. But God is a God who is able to do the impossible, and He changed Mark's heart. That story will come later.

Even though I received my prenatal care from a U.S. government hospital in the Canal Zone, I could have lost this baby, but for the grace of God, due to medical negligence at the time of his birth. Praise God David was born safely in January, 1972. I also praise God for a healthy, good natured baby. David was a cross between Bobby and Mark in his inherited looks and characteristics. And he became the joy of our lives.

Another memorable event was when our car was stolen. It took two weeks and a miracle to recover what was left of it. A Panama Canal Zone Jungle Patrol came across it sitting on a seldom-used, lonely jungle road where the thieves never expected it to be found. They were taking their time methodically stripping it of everything they could salvage and resell. They had already stripped off and taken the rear wheels and the radio, and they had torn out the seats and gas tank, but had not yet hauled them away when the car was found. The rest of the car was intact. Thus we were able to regain the use of the car, but with far less satisfaction. The dash had been torn up as they used a crowbar to tear through the glove compartment and pry out the radio. The seats stunk with a sour smell because they had been left to soak in the tropical rains for over a week. Even so, when it came time to leave Panama for good, God sent us a buyer for this seriously damaged car.

In 1974, by the end of four years at this post, we were more than ready for a change. Our health had begun to deteriorate with multiple allergies and serious problems with molds and fungus. The humidity levels were unbelievable, and I had a constant battle to prevent mildew and rust from destroying all our belongings. Our next post was supposed to be Frankfurt, Germany. We were allowed a full shipment to that country, so all our belongings had been packed up and shipped to Frankfurt before we left for six weeks of home leave.

When we arrived in Fort Walton Beach, Florida, for home leave, we purchased a beautiful, new, bright red Chevy Nova to use while there, and then we would drive it to Washington, D.C., for John's time of consultation. Following that, it would be shipped to Germany for our tour there. But by the end of our home leave, the State Department decided they wanted to send us to Athens, Greece, instead.

Athens was not a full-shipment post, meaning people being sent there would pack most of their belongings for storage and ship only necessities to the post. However, there was no way for us to separate any of our belongings which were already in shipping containers crossing the ocean in route to Frankfurt, from whence they would have to be shipped on to Athens. This meant we had to obtain special waivers to have a full shipment in Athens. Unfortunately, as with many things in the federal bureaucracy, this caused us many headaches down the road, as they later tried to come back and charge us for the extra expense!

Because Athens, at the time of our posting there, had been embroiled in a war with Turkey over the island of Cyprus and because American vehicles were frequently bombed, we were told to bring a "low-profile" vehicle so as not to call attention to ourselves! Unfortunately, our big (by European standards) bright red American car was a far cry from what they were suggesting! Talk about standing out in a crowd! We would have to trust the Lord to protect us.

When our shipment arrived, it was a mess. Everything we owned was covered with sand and mildew. Hangers which had been packed in with clothing had rusted and ruined the clothes. One of our chests of drawers had a hole in the side and a drawer in multiple pieces where a fork lift had crashed through the side of the container. That explained why sand and humidity had infiltrated into everything! I was able to glue the drawer back together, like a jigsaw puzzle, filling multiple cracks with plastic wood. It took hours of scrubbing with bleach solution to get rid of the mold on every surface of the furniture. Some of the rust could not be removed and many items had to be thrown away. Such were some of the joys (!), or should I say misadventures (?), of life in the Foreign Service. We learned to be grateful for even getting our belongings, after hearing horror tales of people who lost everything they owned when their containers were lost at sea.

Our two years in Athens were full of misery. John was traveling out of town almost 70% of the time. The three boys and I suffered from many illnesses. I can remember one occasion when John had been gone for several days on a trip and came home to find me dealing with a very sick little boy. Our 2 1/2-year-old David had a high fever and was coughing constantly. He wouldn't let me put him down. (It turned out he had double pneumonia.) It was extremely cold in the house because the furnace didn't work. Our landlord spoke no English and lived in a city about 200 or 300 miles away! But could John help me with all this? No. There was nothing he could do because he had to leave on another trip the next day! Unfortunately, it wasn't his choice. He had to provide security for our traveling Secretary of State! I must admit I was very angry with our Secretary of State, Mr. Henry Kissinger, at that point! John did contact a Greek national employee of the Embassy who contacted our land-lord in order to get the furnace fixed.

A major problem for us in Greece was that we lived among people with whom we could not communicate. Very few of them spoke any English, and I surely couldn't speak Greek! But they did make a valiant effort to be friendly with us. They took little David in to their homes and stuffed him with fruit and candies just before our dinner hour! (They themselves were hours away from eating.)

There were many aspects of the Greek culture that surprised us. Some of it took a lot of adjustment on our part. It was very strange to us to see all the stores lock their doors and our neighbors shut everything down, put on pajamas, and take naps in the middle of the afternoon! American children who made noise, just as they got out of school in the afternoons, would find themselves facing the police for disturbing the peace! Anyone who flushed a toilet in an apartment building would be in trouble for disturbing the neighbors as the water ran down the sewer pipes inside the walls!

After a long siesta in the afternoon, the Greek nightlife began rather late. Restaurants didn't even open until about 7:30 or 8:00 P.M. (but we usually had our dinner around 5:30), and the parties would go on until 2:00 or 3:00 A.M.. This wasn't helpful for us trying to sleep! It made living there very difficult for us.

We were amazed at how quickly the slightest rude behavior on the streets would bring on a fist fight. And things we would normally do, without giving it a second thought, had to be carefully avoided lest we seriously offend them. This is often true in any foreign culture. It's very important for Americans to learn the social taboos before traveling overseas.

But we did find Greece an awesome place to sightsee. What a thrill to walk the streets that the Apostle Paul walked, to see the place where he was imprisoned in Philippi, to see where he preached at Mars Hill in Athens, and to visit the judgment seat he was dragged before when the Jews got so upset with him in Corinth. We enjoyed seeing the multitudes of archeological sites, ruins of temples and other buildings in historic places all over Greece. That part of being there was fascinating for me because I have always had an interest in archeology. And to be able to visit the many ruins of Athens, Adelphi, Sounion, Corinth, and Philippi, among others, was very awesome.

Another fascinating site to visit was a town called Meteora. The thing that made this place so interesting was the geological formations on which ancient stone monasteries were built. They were very high, enormous rocks with steep sides like cliffs rising 100-300 feet or more on all sides. I don't know of any other place in the world with these unique geological phenomena. The only way to access them originally was to be raised with ropes and pulleys in a net or on a platform. Some of them are still that difficult to reach. But a few have been opened up for visitors and have footbridges and pathways winding up to them.

I learned to really appreciate the saga recorded in Acts of Paul's shipwreck during the storm in the Mediterranean Sea, on his way to Rome for his trial before Caesar. I was constantly amazed at the winds that would blow solidly (without gusting) around my house at gale force, or more, for three or four days straight without letting up. Since our house was up on stilts one floor above the ground, the cold wind would be blowing below us and above us for that length of time. Our polished granite floors would get very cold. If I needed to hang clothes on the line on the roof, I had to be sure to secure them with many clothes-pins and check on them every few minutes to make sure they weren't blown several blocks away. And the clothes would dry super-fast! It certainly made life interesting.

But it also caused me major health problems with my allergies. These winds blew granite dust all over the house from the barren landscape and the quarries around us, where blasting was conducted regularly. Very few people wasted water on lawns in Athens. They would plant flowers, and water only right around the base of the flowers and shrubs or trees, leaving the rest of the yard bare.

Because the only English speaking Baptist church was right outside the American Air Force base, we had a full hour's drive into the heart of the city of Athens and back out again in another direction in order to get to church! And wouldn't you know that our little David would get car sick every time we went anywhere at all! Even a drive to the commissary in the heart of Athens required a bucket for him.

We never felt welcome or accepted in this church. We weren't part of the "clique," being diplomats rather than military! And David couldn't let me out of his sight, so when I went to church I had to sit in the nursery with him. Whenever we missed several Sundays in a row because of sickness (and we were sick a lot) no one ever called to find out why. I got the feeling they didn't care. As a result, I became very hungry for some real fellowship with other Christians and with God. This time in my life was truly a "wilderness" journey.

By the time we were transferred to Nairobi, Kenya, in the summer of 1976, I really needed a new, living, more meaningful relationship with God. I was never so glad to leave a place as I was when we moved from Athens to Nairobi! Thank God we moved after only two years of our three-year assignment! God had truly used this place to break up the hard ground of my heart and prepare it to receive what He wanted to give me in a new place.

Nairobi was a beautiful city.

CHAPTER FIVE

Radical Transformation

Nairobi, Kenya, was a breath of fresh air after the two years in Athens, Greece. It was a study in contrasts between those two cities. Instead of being dry and dusty and barren like Greece, Nairobi was a lush green, filled with exotic plants and animals, and lots of land around the houses. It was truly a beautiful city and we loved it very much.

The boys attended school at the International School of Kenya (ISK). This school was geared for high achievers, those children who wanted to go on to college and pursue higher academic challenges. While our middle son, Bobby, thrived in this environment, our oldest son, Mark, was miserable because he preferred vocational over academic courses. Mark wanted to do things with his hands. That was the only kind of career he was interested in. Because he had never put forth the effort to measure up to his academic potential prior to this, he found himself barely passing. After his first year at ISK we made arrangements for him to return to the states and live with my oldest sister and her husband in Valrico, Florida, where he could attend a school that offered vocational courses. He wanted to be an auto mechanic!

When we arrived in Nairobi, I was spiritually dry and desperately searching for a deeper relationship with God. While on home leave, I had gotten hold of some books giving personal testimonies of how God had touched people's lives in a profound way and filled them with His Spirit, an experience that was called the "Baptism in the Holy Spirit." I began to hunger and thirst for this same touch from God. I started attending a Bible study which was composed almost entirely of missionary wives. I don't have any memory of what we were studying in particular, but they had a lending library and I remember borrowing a book that had a big impact on me. It was Catherine Marshall's book "*Something More, In Search of a Deeper Faith*." That title summed up my deep inner thirst.

Many other books began to shape my faith in a profound way. I came to realize that the God who manifested Himself so powerfully in the Bible was still doing the same things now that He had done then. I heard and read of how He still healed people in miraculous ways. I learned that people today could still speak in "tongues" and could actually hear God talking to them. I heard that the "gifts of the Holy Spirit" exhibited in the New Testament book of Acts — prophecy, word of knowledge, word of wisdom, gifts of healing, and working of miracles — were still being manifested in and through people in the world today. I wanted desperately to know God better and to experience these exciting things for myself!

I began to beg Him for the baptism in the Holy Spirit which Jesus had promised His followers. On one occasion, I remember the thought coming to me that just as I had received Christ as my Savior by faith, and not by <u>feeling</u>, I had to believe that I would receive the baptism in the Holy Spirit by faith and not by feeling. So I prayed one more time and told God that I was not going to ask again. I would believe that I received what I asked for even if I didn't "feel" any different!

In retrospect I can see that was a turning point. I never again doubted that I was a child of God. I had a more profound sense of spiritual security than I had ever had before. And, occasionally, I would have a thought of strange syllables and sounds just rolling off my tongue and a desire to speak them! I had no idea that was God's Spirit leading me to speak in tongues. I remember thinking at the time that I didn't know what those words meant and they could even potentially be curse words that I might have heard in the marketplace. So I kept my mouth shut! Much later I came to realize that the Holy Spirit operates that way in the gift of "speaking in tongues." We do the speaking, but He shapes the utterance.

In Nairobi, I once again found myself teaching adults in Sunday School in the Baptist church we joined. I felt much challenged and somewhat apprehensive to be teaching primarily missionaries along with a few other Americans and Kenyan nationals.

I learned how very important good Christian music is. I had a fairly good selection of music records and tapes. I played the tapes whenever I was in my car, which was a lot. It helped me immensely to not lose my temper in the crazy traffic I encountered. It helped me keep my "cool" whenever I was confronted by difficult circumstances. One day the Indian man who owned the dry-cleaning business I patronized asked me what was so different about me, why I seemed to be at peace all the time. I leaped at the opportunity to tell him it was because I am a Christian.

Nairobi was an exciting place to live. We thoroughly enjoyed the scenery, the climate, and the beauty of this city. Although it was only about 120 miles south of the equator, it was so high in altitude that the temperature was just about perfect. During the dry season the days would be warm, feeling like the high 70's to mid 80's in the sun, with low humidity. But if you walked in the shade it would feel like the 50's or 60's — cool enough to need a sweater! Because the rainy season had less sun, the days would be a little cooler. At night, during either season, it would be in the mid 40's to low 50's.

The city was bejeweled with every imaginable blooming tree and shrub! Jacaranda trees turned the city a beautiful lilac color in their season and left a carpet of flower petals on the streets. Bougainvilleas came in every color imaginable and covered fences and porticoes. Dozens of varieties of flowers bloomed all year long. Some of the trees looked like they were upside down.

And the animals were absolutely fascinating. To drive down the road to any other town or city and see giraffes, baboons, impalas, Grant's gazelles, Thompson's gazelles and other animals roaming near the roads in the wide open was a great thrill. Monkeys would climb all around our hotel room when we stayed in Mombasa or some of the national parks. Lions and cheetahs roamed freely in the land, along with all manner of other wildlife. Lake Nakuru Park was full of flamingoes, and storks, and other kinds of exotic birds and gazelles. And we can't leave out the elephants, hippopotami, rhinoceroses, or thousands of wildebeests and zebras and elands migrating across the land. We loved this place!

I was ashamed to realize, after returning from four years in Kenya, that we had spent most of our time exploring the sights, looking at animals and scenery and all the other adventurous things of this beautiful country. We had almost totally neglected the people of Kenya. And we were so absorbed in our own enjoyment of life there that we never even noticed! We were very selfish at that time.

Sometime during our four years there, between 1976-

1980, we endured an extremely long drought. The rivers dried up, and the lake with the dam which had the hydro-electric generators was so low that the generators were getting clogged with sand. This resulted in rolling black-outs, both scheduled and unscheduled. We would have fore-warning that we would be without power either mornings or afternoons, several different days a week. Quite often, however, there were unexpected blackouts during times when we were supposed to have power.

This also resulted in shortages of all dairy products as the cattle were dying off or not producing milk. Being one of the "elite" foreigners, I could count on the local store-keeper whom I patronized to bring out some of his hoarded stock of milk or butter when I needed it. But he didn't always have it himself, so sometimes we had to do without.

I do remember several ugly events while we were there. One night our family had gone out to dinner and a movie. When we came back to our little dead end street (only about five or six houses on it with ours at the end), there was a crowd of excited Kenyans blocking the road. We locked the car doors in fear of this "mob." Then I heard someone say "It's all right, they live here." They then proceeded to drag a huge chunk of meat off the road with a rope.

Only as they cleared the road did I realize this was a human being tied up on the end of the rope! He had been caught in the act of stealing, and all the guards from all the houses, as well as other servants, had joined in the mob action of beating him with clubs and pangas (a large knife similar to a machete). They had done so thorough a job that he looked like raw meat. We called the police, and he was hauled away to a hospital. Unfortunately he had already lost so much blood that he died.

This was a terrible fact of life in Kenya. It seemed almost all the servants, even public servants, stole in their own way, pilfering from their employers, taking bribes, or whatever.

But anyone who got caught in a public act of stealing would pay the consequences with his life, unless the police were able to intervene before it reached that tragic state. One of our missionary friends had her purse stolen while standing in line at the post office but was afraid to yell "Stop, thief!" because she didn't want to see him beaten to death.

There were many areas in Kenya, as in all our posts, where it was not safe. We were instructed never to wear beads or necklaces of any real value or earrings for pierced ears, unless we had our car windows rolled up and the doors locked. Any time you stopped for traffic, you were fair game for a thief to reach in, grab your purse or jewelry, and run away. They were known to rip earrings right out of the ears! Beggars would line the streets at intersections, asking for money when you stopped for a light.

After two years in Nairobi, we came back to Florida for our first home leave in the summer of 1978. Just before we came back, our "baby" son, David, now six years old, began to express fears about flying on the long trip back to the States. He wanted to know where he would go if the plane crashed and he was killed. I had the joy of leading him to accept Jesus as his personal Savior. I laid hands on him and asked God to fill him with His Holy Spirit. It never occurred to me until years afterward that the sounds I heard him making when no one else was around and he didn't know I was listening might be anything other than childish play. (I still don't know for a fact that he was speaking in tongues, but I strongly suspect it.)

While we were in the States, Mark ended up chauffeuring us around in his graduation present (an old Cadillac). He drove us to Fort Walton Beach to visit John's mother and on out to Texas to visit John's aunt near Dallas. During this time Mark made it very clear how angry he was toward me. His disrespect (in speech) and apparent hostility toward me was very obvious. My heart was breaking while I was there.

After another year (our third) in Kenya, our second son, Bobby, skipped his senior year at the International School and, with the blessings of the principal, went to Florida to attend the University of South Florida at Tampa. He had taken every course of any substance that ISK had to offer, and would be wasting a year to take inconsequential courses like art if he stayed there. He would receive his high school diploma only after successfully completing his freshman year at the University. This was a very difficult year for Bobby because he was not very outgoing and had no desire to be a part of the raucous university scene. But at least he was geographically close to his older brother and to three of my sisters and their families.

Sometime during that last year in Kenya, I attended a seminar in which God opened my eyes to see how I had really messed up in raising Mark. I was stricken to the core and utterly broken by this realization. I immediately repented and asked God's forgiveness. I then began seeking God's help to bring reconciliation between Mark and me.

I prayed for wisdom and, with many tears dripping on the paper, I wrote Mark a letter confessing my wrong and asking his forgiveness. He answered by sending a letter to his dad (on the outside of which he wrote: "for Dad's eyes only"). He asked his dad to tell me not to write to him any more. This really tore me up. I kept trying, but never got a response. (I was told later by Bobby that Mark would tear up my letters and throw them in the trash.)

When we got ready to return to the states for an assignment in Washington, I asked all my missionary friends to pray for me and my son, that God would tear down the walls and bring forgiveness and true reconciliation.

Going first to Florida for home leave, we met Mark's fiancée, Christine. I was dismayed to see the way he would walk all over her and treat her so terribly. I knew that Chris had been raised by her father and stepmother in a broken and dysfunctional home. I knew she was nominally a Catholic but had no real relationship with Jesus. I knew she never attended church nor was she taught in the ways of God.

I began praying for Chris' salvation, as well as for Mark's return to the Lord. I began praying that God would intervene and cause them to break up if their marriage was not God's will for them. I particularly asked God that, if they were right for each other in His will, He would bring Chris to salvation and bring Mark to rededicate his life to Jesus before they got married.

When we moved into a rental home in Springfield, Virginia, we began trying all the Baptist churches around, praying God would show us where he wanted us to belong. One day a woman called from one of these churches, and I asked her if they had anyone who was holding a neighbor-hood Bible study. She said no, but there was someone named Tommie who formerly attended their church and who was interested in starting one.

Later that day I got a phone call from Tommie. She wanted to start a Bible study but didn't know how. Tommie and I hit it off like long-lost friends! We ended up talking on the phone that first day for about four hours straight. We had lots of things in common, starting with the fact we each had three sons and were having very similar problems with them. We decided to get together just to pray for our kids. She invited another friend named Sue who also had three sons and similar problems, and we started meeting on Thursday mornings at Tommie's house. After the first or second meeting there were six or eight who heard about it and wanted to come also.

By the second meeting we decided to add Bible study to our prayer time, and I reluctantly agreed to teach it. My primary hesitation was that I didn't have all of my shipment, including all my Bible reference books. Furthermore, half our stuff was still in boxes waiting to be unpacked and put away! Within two or three weeks we had at least a dozen people there every week. God began moving in our midst and answering prayers like none of us had ever experienced before. We were all getting excited.

God began answering my prayers for Mark and Chris. It wasn't long before Mark called me, and he was in tears. He wanted his dad's work number so he could talk to him. I asked him what was wrong, and he said Chris had left him! He wanted to talk to his dad, not to me.

After I got off the phone, I was suddenly filled with guilt. Guilt because I had prayed that God would somehow cause them to break up if this marriage was not right for them. And grief because my son was devastated! This was the first time I had heard him cry in many years. This is the son who had such a hard heart he would never let me see him cry when I spanked him! But as I was feeling so guilty, I suddenly realized that God had put that prayer in my heart and He would not have answered it had it not been according to His will. So I rejoiced that God was at work, even though my heart was breaking because my son was in such pain.

Not long after that, Mark called and asked me to give him salvation Scriptures to give to Chris. I could hardly believe my ears! This boy — who had slept with her, had done drugs with her, and had never indicated in any way that he might be a Christian — now wanted to show her how to be saved!?! I asked if she had indicated a desire to know how to be saved. "Of course not," he responded, but he was going to tell her anyway! I asked very gently if he hadn't been upset with me because I had tried to jam religion down his throat and how would Chris like it if he did the same thing to her, but he wouldn't be dissuaded. So I gave him the Scripture references.

It turned out that Chris was frightened half out of her wits when Mark started doing this. She thought he had gone crazy! She and her family, believing themselves to be in danger from Mark, decided she should move somewhere else and not let him know how to get in touch with her. I continued to pray for her salvation and to rejoice that my son was beginning to turn back to the Lord. He even admitted to me that we had raised him right! I never expected to ever hear any such statement from him.

After about a year, and at a time when Mark was being pulled and twisted and tormented by another girl whom he was dating, Chris wrote to me to tell me she had accepted Christ as her Savior. She didn't know why she was writing to me, but I quickly wrote back and told her it was because I had been praying for her salvation. I rejoiced in another answered prayer and the salvation of this lovely girl from such a messed up home.

She asked us not to give her address to Mark. But while we were away one evening, Mark called, and Bobby, not knowing he shouldn't, told Mark we had gotten a letter from her and proceeded to give him her address and phone number! Within a week, they were engaged again and attending church together! Talk about miracles!

God brought Chris up from Florida to visit us in Virginia a few months later. While John and I were sitting with her on the sofa going through some picture albums, the Holy Spirit fell on us all and filled us with such love for each other that we always felt, from that moment on, that she was our real, natural-born daughter. In fact, it seemed more like she was our daughter and Mark, our son-in-law, rather than the other way around! And she has let me know many times over the years that she feels more like I'm her Mom than her real mother is. That's how God can move to "set the lonely in families," as He says in His word! (Psalm 68:6)

To make a long story short, after many ups and downs, Chris and Mark were married. They've had lots of problems and hardships and lots of growing experiences over the years since then. I've had an ongoing mentoring relationship with Chris during all those years, and God has used me on many occasions to minister in some special way to her. It's certainly not a typical relationship between a woman and her daughter-in-law.

Now Mark and Chris are both committed to serve the Lord. They are involved in a wonderful full gospel church in their town near Atlanta, Georgia, and have three teenage sons who are giving them just as much trouble, if not more, than our boys had given us. Over the years God has torn down those walls around Mark's heart and put a genuine love in his heart for me! Hallelujah!

But back to my story about our Bible study that the Lord had put together. God was really moving and answering prayers going and coming, and we were all excited. However, John kept me in turmoil with complaints about my being gone too much. At that time I thought he was complaining about my housekeeping. I worked as hard as I could to be a super-wife and mother. I made sure the house was spotless and all the washing and ironing done so he wouldn't have a valid complaint about my activities. But the expressions of resentment continued. I felt like I was being persecuted.

I know now that it was a problem for him that he could never reach me on the phone because I was either out somewhere, or else I was on the phone for hours at a time and he would keep getting a busy signal. (That was before we had an answering machine or call-waiting or cell phones.) Also, in retrospect, I came to believe that John was jealous and afraid he was going to lose me because I had something special in my relationships with my Bible study friends that he didn't have.

One day after I had been out shopping and had been working really hard around the house, John called and asked if he could bring some people by for coffee and cake after supper. I was exhausted, and that was the last thing on earth that I wanted to do, but because he persisted I finally agreed. So I had to bake a cake and fix dinner, then get things cleaned up quickly after supper so they could find a clean house when they came by.

This was how I met Jean Norment from Montgomery, Alabama. She was with her husband when he had come up to see John on business at the Department of State. They were Christians and owned a glass company that made bulletproof glass for prisons and other facilities. He had been praying for a long time for God to help him sell his glass to the Department of State for our embassies.

At the same time, God had brought John back to the states at a crucial moment in history, after our embassy had been taken over by a mob in Iran and after several of our embassies had been bombed. John was in charge of a new effort to establish greater security standards, find better security products to keep people from being able to get into our embassies so quickly, and minimize damage from truck bombs. He was working with various companies helping them develop products that would meet the needs of the Department of State.

So John was able to help Bobby Norment understand why he couldn't sell just glass, and to see that he needed to produce a whole entrance-way product with his glass in it — one that was able to withstand whatever assault people threw at it for a certain length of time — before he could hope to sell it to the Department of State.

Jean would come up with her husband from time to time, and we spent a few hours together each time. It seemed that God ordained for her to show up every time I was discouraged or hurting in my marriage relationship or because of the kids. We would talk and she would pray with me. She was the one God brought into my life to minister to me for over a year. During that time He revealed to me more deeply than I had ever known how very much He loved me, and ultimately He set me free from a lifelong oppression by a spirit of rejection and condemnation.

Several months after that initial meeting with the Norments, we went through Montgomery, Alabama, on our way to visit John's mother in Fort Walton Beach, Florida. We stopped in Montgomery over the weekend, and visited with the Norments. I went to church with Jean at her Assembly of God church on that Sunday night. I had never attended a Pentecostal- type church before, though I had often wanted to.

At the end of the service, the pastor gave one of those all-inclusive invitations where everyone had to come forward toward the altar. That left most of us tightly packed into the aisles with no place to go. But as we stood there, a message in tongues came forth from one side of the building and then an interpretation from the other. This was a message of encouragement that seemed tailor-made for me. But my analytical mind persuaded my heart that the particular message could have been for many different people. So I prayed silently: "Lord, if that message was for me, could you give me another?"

Immediately, from the choir loft directly ahead, there came a prophetic message that zinged into my heart and I knew that I knew that I knew it was for me! It was an invitation to come to God and receive all that He had to give. Oh, how I wanted to do just that! My heart was pounding, and I had a battle raging in my soul. Fear overcame me, and I stayed rooted to the spot. I'm sure my friend Jean was praying for me as we stood side by side in that aisle.

Years later I came to realize that all of my life I had hesitated from acting upon, or struggled against what God was speaking to me, or asking me to do, out of fear of what others would think. The Bible says *"Fear of man will prove to be a snare"* (Prov. 29:25). Fear of what my father would think had held me captive and prevented me from openly confessing to the church that I was receiving Jesus as my Savior. Fear of my husband had kept me from speaking prophetic words that God gave me for the church on many occasions. Fear of what my family would say, fear of being rejected by them, kept me for six to eight months from responding to God's call to preach the gospel. Fear had kept me for six months from answering God's call to start an Aglow chapter and be its first president after God had shown me clearly that was what He was asking of me.

On this particular occasion, I stood there immovable, waiting for the moment I could escape from this church. I was thrilled with the call of God to "come and receive," but afraid to answer it. When we went on down to visit "Mom" in Florida, she revealed to me that she had wanted on many occasions to put her arms around me and tell me she loved me, but I had an invisible wall up. I acknowledged that I knew that, and said God was changing me. I had no idea how prophetic that word was. God was indeed getting ready to tear that wall down! I praise God for setting me free about five months later!

In the meantime, there was one other occasion when God used Jean in a very special way to impact my life. John had told me Bobby Norment was coming up for a week and that Jean was coming with him. I began to get excited, looking forward to seeing her and hoping to be able to show her around and spend some time with her. However, when their arrival date came and went, I didn't hear anything from them. After a couple of days I called Bobby at his hotel and asked if Jean had come. He told me she had been too busy and had decided to stay home.

But suddenly out of the blue, a day or two later, I was told she was coming after all, and she showed up the following day! I was overjoyed and sat talking with her on my sofa during the afternoon while a standing rib roast was cooking in my oven for her and Bobby that night. When I asked her how long she was going to be in town, she blew me out of the water with her answer.

"Oh, I'm going back home tomorrow. I just came up to have dinner with you tonight" she said. "I wasn't planning to come up at all because I was teaching a special series and ... (this and that) ...," she explained. "Then Bobby called and told me to come on up, but I was too busy. But God said 'Go on up there, Jean.' So I came on up." It seems the night I had called Bobby, he heard the disappointment in my voice and called her to come. Yet she wouldn't have come unless God had told her to.

I was totally unprepared for that answer. I just began sobbing. It hit me like a ton of bricks that God told her to drop all her good works and get a plane ticket (which I knew probably cost at least a thousand dollars) to fly up to Washington just to have dinner with me! That God loved me enough to do that, and that Jean loved me that much, just blew me away!

Needless to say, that prepared the way for God to use Jean for my life-changing deliverance in January,1982, just a few months later, as described in chapter one.

CHAPTER SIX

God's Supernatural Ways

A short while before God brought me deliverance and emotional healing through Jean Norment, I had a very strange experience. I was still teaching my neighborhood Bible study at the time. In addition, John and I were involved with a military couples Bible study group called Officers' Christian Fellowship. Several of the women in my Bible study came to this same group with their husbands, which is why John and I had been included even though we were not military! We would take turns having the meetings at our homes and whoever was the host or hostess would usually teach the Bible Study.

On one occasion, when we met at our house, I decided to teach on speaking in tongues, showing how it can be either from demons or from the Holy Spirit. After the meeting was over that evening, and John and I had gone to bed, I lay tossing and turning, struggling in vain to go to sleep. After a couple of hours I was beginning to feel really bad. All of a sudden, probably about 2:00 A.M., the curtain rod on the window near my side of the bed came crashing down! In the natural, there is absolutely no way this curtain rod could have fallen by itself. It was a café-style rod, the type you have to lift up in order to unhook it from a prong on top of the wall bracket if you want to take it down. There was no curtain on this rod, and neither of the support brackets had come down. The rod was left hanging on one end while the other end was hanging toward the floor.

I immediately understood that there was a battle going on in the room between unseen spirits, angels versus demons! I got up, went to the bathroom, and began praying and binding the evil spirits in the name of Jesus. Then I was able to go to sleep.

The next morning I called a Spirit-filled friend and told her about this incident. She suggested I call a friend of hers, Billie Deck, and ask her to come over and "cleanse" my house spiritually. I did this and Billie came over at the agreed-upon time, along with a couple of my closest friends. She gave us instructions in line with what God had shown her to do, and we went through the house praying and anointing the windows and doors with oil.

There were several items we had brought back from other countries that Billie felt may have given evil spirits an opening into our home. One was a replica of a pagan god. I got rid of that idol replica and as many of the other things as possible, and asked God to sanctify the rest. She also told me she sensed something demonic in my son Bobby's room. When I mentioned this to him later, he took out some evil looking posters, along with some hard rock music tapes, and destroyed them outside on our grill. We didn't have any more "visitations" after that.

Shortly after my supernatural deliverance, God arranged, through the State Department, to send John out of town for a few weeks. While he was gone, I read a book called *Love Life for Every Married Couple*, by Dr. Ed Wheat, that opened my eyes and ultimately transformed my marriage. I realized what a lousy wife I had been to my husband all those years. (At one point we had even discussed divorce because we were so miserable.) I came to the place where I could humble myself before John when he returned. I asked him to forgive me for having been such a terrible wife and promised that with God's help I would work on changing.

One of the things God revealed to me was the fact that John and I were living as two separate individuals rather than being united in heart and purpose. There was a serious breakdown in communication between us. There was very little that we shared in terms of interests. I came to realize that I needed to make the effort to try to spend more time with him and to learn to communicate.

I started taking walks around the block with him, which he had been asking me to do for a long time, but I had not really desired to do. Over a short period of time, John began to open up more and more to me about the things he was involved in at work, issues about which he needed to talk with someone who would listen. I was gradually able to begin sharing the spiritual things that were becoming so very important to me. This was another start on the way to healing our marriage.

Another thing God taught me during this time was to stop talking so much and learn to listen. I, like many others, had great difficulty dealing with silent moments. If nothing was going on or being said, I felt compelled to fill the silence with my own words. This is a very effective way to keep others from talking. I asked God to put a guard on my mouth and tongue and to help me to keep silent except when He wanted me to speak. I learned from God how to begin to listen to others, including my husband.

I gradually learned how God speaks to me personally. I am one who normally receives God's voice through the Scriptures. A particular passage will leap out at me. Or a verse or passage will suddenly come into my mind with a sense of excitement or urgency. Sometimes it will be a random thought and a sudden conviction that this is from God. Sometimes it's just a simple thought that I presume to be my own. Many times, but not always, my heart will start pounding or I have a "sense" of excitement inside when God is speaking to me, either by a thought or a Scripture verse. Sometimes God speaks to me through circumstances, or through other people.

Several months after my deliverance, I went into a Christian book store looking for a book. What I was searching for was not there, but I found something far more valuable. The woman who ran that store never let anyone come and go without praying for them. As she started to pray for me she suddenly stopped and said, "Oh! I see a huge wing! It's the wing of God! And He's sweeping people into your heart! He's going to bring many people into your life and He's going to give you a ministry of great love."

As I left that store, I was overwhelmed with awe. On the way home I was listening to a song on the car radio by Bill Gaither that says something like this: "I am loved, you are loved, I can risk loving you; we are free to love each other, we are loved." I suddenly remembered (I know the Holy Spirit brought this to my mind) the words in 2 Corinthians 12:9-10 where Paul said he rejoiced in his weaknesses because when he was weak then he would be strong. He meant that God's power would come through and would enable him to be strong in those weaknesses. I marveled that God planned to use me in a ministry of love, because that had been my greatest weakness! And I wept and worshiped God all the way home.

A year or two after God had used Jean to deliver me from demonic oppression, I woke up from the most vivid dream of my life. It was so fresh in my mind and there was such awe in my soul, that I knew that I knew it was from God. I dreamed I was walking toward a building that looked like a school and met a couple with a small child coming toward me. The child suddenly collapsed. I put my hands on his head and prayed and then walked on. Later (in the dream) I learned that the child had been dying of cancer, but God had healed him when I prayed. After I awoke, I had a sense of "knowing" that God wanted to use me in a ministry of healing.

This dream thrilled me to the core for days, and weeks, and even for months afterward, every time I thought of it. But I knew deep in my heart that I wasn't ready for such a ministry. Not only that, I knew I wasn't even willing to let God use me in a ministry like that. I confessed this to God (not that He didn't already know my heart), but I told Him I was willing for Him to change my heart and prepare me for such a ministry.

In the years since that dream, God has indeed prepared me. And He put within my heart an earnest desire to be used of Him not only to heal people physically, but also to heal them emotionally and spiritually, to bring deliverance to the oppressed, and to bring many souls into His kingdom. He has already used me to do some of that. But I believe that I have hardly begun to fulfill the dream God put in my heart. I also know that it's only by His grace and mercy and not my own doing that any of this has already come to pass.

On another occasion when John was overseas on a temporary trip, I woke up about 2:00 A.M. and could not go back to sleep. I am normally a very sound sleeper, and can usually fall asleep again very easily when I do awaken. But this time I struggled in vain to go back to sleep, tossing and turning, and began to feel really dreadful. Finally, I had the thought (I now realize it was from the Holy Spirit) that perhaps God wanted me to pray for someone. I resigned myself to forfeit the sleep I so deeply craved and said, rather grudgingly, "Okay, Lord. Who do you want me to pray for?"

Instantly the phone on the chest of drawers on the other side of my bed rang!

Now wide awake, I climbed out of bed and answered the phone. A woman who had attended our Bible Study regularly for about a year before moving (a couple of years earlier) to Atlanta, was on the other end apologizing for waking me up. I was surprised to hear myself say, under the anointing of the Holy Spirit, "You didn't wake me up. God woke me up about a half hour ago."

She said, "You're kidding. Are you serious? I don't believe that."

I said, "Yes, it's true. I've been tossing and turning, and trying to go back to sleep for half an hour. And I had just asked God who He wanted me to pray for when the phone rang."

"That's how long I've been dialing your number part way through and hanging up! I can't believe God woke you up then," she said.

"What's wrong?" I asked.

I'll never forget the answer she gave me: "I want you to tell me why I shouldn't kill myself."

"Tell me why you think you should" came tumbling out of my mouth, as I desperately began to pray silently in the Spirit and listen to her tale of woe. I knew in my inmost being that she was deadly serious.

During the course of the conversation, she told me everything she had done to destroy her marriage and how her husband had walked out and filed for divorce. She revealed that she was sitting there drinking, trying to get up the nerve to kill herself and her little girl, who was sleeping on the sofa near her!

I can't tell you the rest of the conversation, but I remember feeling totally inadequate for this task God had dropped in my lap. I remember feeling cold, emotionally and physically. The room temperature was in the 60's and I didn't have my robe on, nor did I dare ask her to wait while I got up and put one on (we didn't have cordless phones then). I remember feeling frustrated with her, knowing she had never listened to my advice before, and feeling it was a useless exercise to tell her the same things over again, yet knowing there was nothing else I could say to her anyway.

I didn't "feel" the Holy Spirit moving through me for most of the conversation, like I sometimes had, as I spoke. On the contrary, I felt like my words were utterly empty and powerless. Yet God used them to touch and change her heart! After about two hours of this, she said: "Well, I think I can go to sleep now." And she said goodbye and hung up.

As soon as she hung up, the enormity of what had just happened hit me and I began to shake all over. There was no sleep for me the rest of that night! Nor could I forget that episode for a long time to come. I was in awe over how God had used me, when I felt so helpless and useless, to save this woman's life and that of her daughter.

He had also taught me another lesson in my spiritual journey. We walk by faith, not by our "feelings." If I had gone by my feelings, I would have given up on her and not even tried to help. It doesn't matter whether we can feel God's Spirit using us or speaking through us. We just have to speak whatever comes to mind and believe the Holy Spirit is putting the words in our mouth when the need arises, whether we can "feel"Him or not. After all, that's what He promises to do! I've had people tell me on many occasions that God was speaking through me to their heart, when I thought I was just talking!

Sometime later, right after my son's wedding in Florida, I had an occasion to drop by and visit her in Atlanta on my way back from Florida. We had a wonderful visit then, as I was able to share my testimony of what God had done for me and minister to her. She said I looked five to ten years younger than I had before, and she was right. God had taken many years of heaviness and darkness off my face when He set me free.

After God's powerful work of deliverance and transformation in my life, I began to think about my oldest brother Lee who was already in the military before I was old enough to remember. He had come out of the service and gone to college at the University of Florida while I was very young, so I have only short memories of any activities or interaction with him. I knew he wasn't a Christian, and I had been praying over the years for him and his children to somehow come to know Jesus, but really knew nothing about any of the children, other than their names. I wanted very much to share with Lee what God had done for me.

And so I began praying for an opportunity to witness to him. I had no idea how or where this might happen, because I hadn't seen Lee in at least twenty years. He lived in New York state, and we never saw or spoke to one another!

When my oldest son Mark and his fiancée Chris got married, they chose to have their wedding at my oldest sister Mildred's house. She had a showcase garden in her back yard in central Florida, and Mark had lived with them during his last two years of high school. On the day of the wedding, in early June, 1984, John and I, and my mother-in-law, along with our other sons Bob and David, were down there for the wedding.

Right after Mark and Chris left for their honeymoon, who should walk in but my brother Lee with two of his grown kids? He had no idea we were there or that my son had gotten married in Mildred's back yard that very day! He just "happened" to be vacationing at Daytona Beach and decided to come over and visit Mildred. God certainly works in mysterious ways, His wonders to perform.

Later in the evening, after supper, we were all sitting in Mildred's large living room talking, and somehow the subject got around to religion and I had my opportunity for which I had prayed for many months! I shared from my heart the goodness of God and what He had done for me!

On this occasion, I could feel God's anointing on me as I spoke and Lee was thirsty, drinking it in. But he would not come to a point of decision. He diverted the issue to those difficult questions that unbelievers like to throw out, such as "If God is in charge, and He's a good God, then why is there such evil in the world and why do bad things like tornadoes or earthquakes happen?"

Before I could open my mouth, Mildred jumped in with a standard "religious" answer. It was amazing to watch Lee's face as he looked at her with impatience, waiting for me to give him an answer. While Mildred was speaking, I prayed. As soon as she finished God gave me an amazing answer. The evening went on like this until it was obvious we had said all we could say, and Lee was resisting the Holy Spirit, refusing to take that step of accepting Christ!

Among other things in this situation, I learned with amazement that God had answered my prayers over the years for Lee's children. They were all professing Christians. I could rejoice in that knowledge, while continuing to pray for Lee's salvation. I have since that time had other opportunities to witness to him under the Holy Spirit's anointing, but as far as I know now, twenty years later, he has not yet made a commitment to Jesus. But only God knows his heart.

A friend named Alice Holland, from our Officer's Christian Fellowship, took me under her wing and began taking me to retreats from time to time with a group called Women's Aglow Fellowships, International. (They have since changed their name to "Aglow International.") I very much enjoyed those times! It was such a thrill to experience the presence of the Lord in the times of worship and ministry, to see occasional physical healings or deliverances, and to see God moving in other ways in people's lives. He was certainly changing mine in powerful ways!

In our new non-denominational church, we had a friend

named Leslie who was dying from liver cancer. Our church believed in all the gifts of the Spirit, including healing, and often prayed for her in the public worship service. Her husband Skip had a serious problem at first trying to believe God could heal his wife.

One Friday, I was taking Leslie to an appointment and she began telling me how Skip had broken his arm the day before. It was a serious total break of his forearm near the elbow. The doctors had removed a large amount of blood with a syringe. But, because of the swelling, they had put it in a sling, intending to put it in a cast when he returned on Monday, if the swelling had gone down.

As she began telling me how it happened, God put in my heart that He was going to heal Skip so he would be able to believe for his wife's healing! I laughed out loud with joy. I'm sure Leslie thought I had gone crazy, laughing at her husband's misfortune, until I told her God had shown me He was going to heal Skip! I don't know whether she believed me or not, but she was polite enough not to openly challenge what I said.

The following Sunday morning, during the worship time, a prophetic word came forth that God was there to heal people of various things. There was a call for "body ministry." This meant that anyone who needed healing would stand up, then all who had it in their hearts to pray for a certain person would gather around that person, lay hands on them, and pray. I immediately made a beeline for Skip, as did many others in the church. I was standing behind him and put my hand on his back and began praying in the Spirit. I had no doubt God was going to heal Skip. I felt a great amount of heat going through Skip as we prayed and fully believed God was healing his arm.

Later, during the sermon, I watched Skip using that same arm to take notes, even erasing things he had written! With great joy in my heart I thought to myself: "God has healed that arm!" The following evening he and Leslie came to our Officer's Christian Fellowship meeting at our home. Sure enough, he had a tale to tell!

He had gone back to Walter Reed Hospital that morning to get the cast put on his arm. They x-rayed it first to make sure the bone was in the right position, and the x-ray technician and doctors thought they had made a mistake. They went back and took more x-rays and couldn't believe their eyes. The "before" view, taken at the end of the previous week, showed clearly that the bone of his forearm was completely broken. The "after" view, taken on Monday morning, showed no evidence the bone had ever been broken! God didn't supernaturally heal the broken bone in a speeded-up fashion. He made it as though it had never been broken! Skip still has the x-rays to prove it.

The saga of Leslie and her liver cancer lasted many years with many ups and downs. For reasons none of us could understand, she gradually grew worse. One day when she was in the hospital, wasted away to skin and bones, almost comatose and at death's door, Alice and I went to see her. Before we left for the hospital, we met at my house and prayed for a long time. God spoke something to us that we interpreted to mean He was going to heal her. We went to the hospital with that expectation. But she was in great distress and wanting to die. In effect, she told us good-bye. I clung to God's promise to heal her, except for one moment the next day when I suddenly thought of how much she was suffering. I know now that this was God's Spirit preparing me. It wasn't long until I got the word that she had gone to be with the Lord.

I was devastated. So was everyone else in the church. I couldn't understand it. I just knew God had told me He was going to heal her! Of course, heaven is the ultimate healing. But that wasn't my understanding of what He was going to do. I struggled for at least two weeks, demanding to know why God had not healed her. I was angry with God.

Then in church one Sunday morning during the worship time, God spoke a very hard word to me. He said, "Stop asking me <u>why</u>. You just want to know <u>who is to blame</u>. My ways are above your ways and my thoughts are above your thoughts. Your place is to pray with faith and to leave the rest with me. It's not your responsibility whether the sick will be healed or not."

As soon as God had said that to me, the pastor's wife gave a prophetic word that in essence said the same thing to the congregation. I realized God was speaking the truth about my motives. I had been questioning whether <u>we</u> didn't have enough faith, whether <u>she</u> didn't have enough faith, whether there was undisclosed sin in Leslie's life or in our lives (that would perhaps explain why we didn't see our prayers answered). Seeing my sin, I repented, and asked God to forgive me.

I learned a hard lesson through all this. The "faith" movement often puts a heavy guilt trip on people with major problems. The teaching that God always wants to heal, that He will heal if we meet certain conditions, that we have to have faith and hold on to His promises, and that we have to repent of all sin in our lives, while certainly containing Biblical truth, does not leave any room for God's sovereignty. It puts the burden on <u>us</u> to make the healing happen. In fact, it makes us move into presumption and arrogance in telling God — no, <u>demanding</u> that God do what He promises!

Leslie had felt guilty and condemned because she was somehow never able to be healed when the church was putting such emphasis on this. She was made to feel like it was her fault, yet she had done everything she knew to do to "receive" God's promised healing! We had no intention of putting her under condemnation, but that was the effect our faith and public prayers often had on her. I pray that God will stop me short if I ever again start praying out of my petty understanding and without making room for God's sovereign decision to do differently than I might expect! But I also want to be able to truly pray in faith for God's healing when I see people suffering.

On another occasion, God suddenly opened my eyes to see something about myself that I had not realized before. He showed me that he had called me as a young teenager to preach the Gospel. But because of my own particular background and culture I didn't think women could preach in America. So I had immediately, subconsciously changed the call to one of becoming a missionary, thinking perhaps if I were a missionary I could preach overseas.

When I realized God was calling me to preach, I felt, once again, overwhelmed with fear. My first thought was "Oh no! Lord, you couldn't want me to do that. You just set me free from rejection and now you want me to do something that will bring it on again?" I just knew that if I accepted the call to preach the Gospel, my family would reject me. I also wondered if my husband would reject me. This was a very big fear for me. I struggled for several months and then said "yes" to God. But I had no idea when, where, how, or what I needed to do to prepare for such a ministry. So I laid it before the Lord and expected Him to show me when the right time came. Several years passed before He clarified what the next step would be.

Meanwhile, I was going happily on my way to a life of ministry, counseling people, setting captives free, and bringing emotional and occasionally physical healing to people. I thought I knew the direction God was taking me. I got involved with Aglow, first by attending meetings and retreats, and then I began to have a desire to serve as a prayer counselor in the outreach meetings.

But God caught me by surprise one day. I was sitting in a meeting during an Aglow Retreat, worshiping God during the time of praise and worship, when I suddenly had a mental picture of a large geographical area, like a map of part of northern Virginia, and the realization that there was no Aglow group there. Simultaneously I felt in my heart that there were hundreds of women who had to work just to afford to live in that area. I realized they needed an evening Aglow. And I also knew, somehow, that God wanted me to start one and be the first President. All of this came to me in a moment's time. I can't begin to tell you how frightening that thought was! I had never served in any office in this ministry, and suddenly God tells me he wants me to start a chapter and serve as President!

My immediate response was "No, Lord." What an oxymoron. If God is Lord, we can't tell Him "no." Obviously, at that moment, I wasn't allowing God to be my Lord! Rather, I was giving in to fear. Immediately after that, God shut down every form of ministry I was involved in. For instance, the calls I had been receiving for counseling (several times a week) suddenly stopped coming.

It took about six months before I was brought to a place of repentance and acceptance of God's call to start a new evening Aglow for working women. It scares me when I realize how close I came to missing out on God's will for my life. If I had continued to say "no," He would have used someone else to fulfill His plan (in fact, she was already prepared for that very thing and told me so), and I would have missed the blessing. This new chapter, called the Springfield Evening Aglow, began in January, 1986.

Aglow is a wonderful ministry for training women to be leaders in ministry. Many women pastors came up through the ranks of Aglow. The dynamics of relationships on a leadership team for an Aglow Lighthouse, or committee, or Area Team can lead to lots of problems, but also lots of spiritual growth. It just depends on the individuals involved, and how they each respond to the pressures and frictions.

One occasion caused me extreme heartache and pain. I was asked to serve on the selection committee for our next Area Board president. I had been perfectly happy with our current president and had no desire to see anyone else in that position. But at our first committee meeting, someone said, right at the beginning of our meeting, that there was no one else who could serve except the current president. Suddenly the thought came to my mind, and I blurted it out loud, that my friend Alice Holland was a very good prospect! Alice immediately jumped up and left the room in turmoil. Another woman on the Area Board angrily asked me if someone had put me up to that suggestion. The meeting had to be adjourned and rescheduled for another time since I had just nominated Alice, and she could not be present for the committee meeting if her name was in the pot.

I didn't realize the Area Board had been divided over this very issue, and I had jumped squarely in the middle of a serious problem. I learned later that Alice had been encouraged by another member of the Area Board to run for this position and had steadfastly refused. She had finally told the Lord she would let her name go into the hat only if someone else nominated her!

At the next meeting of the committee, things were done in such a way that the current president was re-selected in what I considered to be a very improper way. While I had not been set on seeing my friend put into that position, I did expect to have an opportunity to talk about the issue of one candidate versus the other before we voted. But we had a quick prayer, and one vote was taken without any discussion being permitted. Then the result was accepted immediately with a one vote majority, without any effort to come to unity!

To understand the effect this had on me, you need to realize that the Area Board was over the local chapters in organizational structure and authority. And when they held training sessions for local chapter leaders, they always emphasized the need for striving to arrive at unanimous decisions, especially on issues that were important. As far as I could see, the Area Team wasn't following its own rules which they had so deeply ingrained in me on how to come to decisions! And this devastated me!

This deep wound festered in me for months. I did everything I knew to forgive the Area Board, especially the one who was chairing the committee. I asked God to forgive her and them and tried to let go of this pain in my heart. All without success. I cried at the drop of a hat. I was struggling to deal with this alone because I wasn't permitted to speak to anyone about it, not even to the members of my own local board! My friend was equally wounded, thinking I had voted against her, because she couldn't imagine the selection process not being unanimous. And I couldn't tell her how the meeting had been conducted or the decision made.

After several months of this struggle, I was in an Area Board-sponsored seminar where the speaker was Dottie Schmitt, the same woman who had been speaking at the retreat when God had called me to start an evening Aglow! She talked about John the Baptist as he sat in the dungeon, and the question he asked Jesus (through his disciples), *"Are you the one who was to come, or should we expect someone else?"*(Luke 7:20) Then Jesus pointed out the work He was doing (which fulfilled the prophecy of the Messiah in Isaiah 61:1-3) and concluded His answer with the statement, *"blessed is he whosoever should not be offended in me"* (John 7:23 KJV) She explained that the problem John had was that Jesus wasn't doing what John had expected him to do! And under John's circumstances, he was beginning to doubt Jesus really was the Messiah.

The moment she uttered this explanation, the Holy Spirit opened my eyes to see why I was still struggling with the matter of forgiving the Area Board. The truth was I was really offended in God! I hadn't realized that at the time. I had expected God to do what He had revealed to me, i.e., put my friend Alice into the presidency of the Area Board. And God did not do what I expected him to. I was really angry with God and hadn't realized it! I immediately repented with many tears, and released my anger and asked for God's forgiveness. From that day on, my pain was gone, the forgiveness was complete, and I was at peace again.

I realized many years later that sometimes God reveals something to us that will take place in the future, but we get out of His timing in seeking to see it fulfilled. Alice was selected to be the President of the Area Board at the end of that particular term when it was time for the selection to be made again. Since that time the whole process has changed and Aglow leaders are no longer chosen in that way.

We had one person on our local Springfield Evening executive board who seemed to have her own agenda. It took me many hours on my face before the Lord, on many occasions, in order to deal with her. And even at that, I made many mistakes, which caused her to really get angry with me. The leaders of our Area Board, who had the oversight of all the chapters, had to intervene at one point, leading to great heartbreak. But God showed me the real instigator of the problem was our enemy Satan. And he was having a field day! I reached out to her in love, and God began a healing process that was probably not totally finished when I was transferred overseas.

I also learned how violently the devil is opposed to the Aglow ministry. I saw over and over again how he came against us in many different ways. I saw individuals who were doing just fine in their lives until the very moment they agreed to take some position in this ministry. Then bam! They got hit with multiple problems working to dissuade them from the course they had chosen. Some gave in to the pressure and backed away. Others recognized the source of the problem and trusted God to enable them to overcome.

Praise God, He allows the tests to strengthen His children, and He gives the victory to those who trust Him!

About nine months after this new Aglow chapter had been launched, my husband and I decided it was time to change churches. We visited an Assembly of God (A/G) church and we both knew on the first Sunday that this was the church we were looking for. That was also the day I learned about the Assemblies of God correspondence school for people preparing for ministry who couldn't go to college. God began to stir again in me the desire to preach, and He showed me He wanted me to send off to the Berean Bible College for a ministry preparation course.

Still I dragged my feet, until one of the women on my local Aglow Executive Board called me and told me God told her He wanted me to enroll in some college classes. I realized this was confirmation of what God had already put in my heart. After consulting with our District Secretary about the requirements of the Assemblies of God for getting ministerial credentials with them, I finally sent off for my first study course.

Although God took me through many trials and tests as the president of the Springfield Evening Aglow, it was a time of tremendous growth with joy and blessing and fulfill-ment. I've learned that Aglow is an amazing vehicle for God's training in ministry. The difficulties that often have to be worked out in relationships between various board members are only one aspect of the learning process. It's an excellent place to learn self-discipline, as well as how to pray and minister to others.

God used this time of service to open doors for ministry that I would never have known how to open myself. One such door that He supernaturally opened was a once-a-month church service for the women incarcerated in the Fairfax Adult Detention Center. Prior to this, God had begun stirring in my heart a desire to minister in the jail, but

I had no idea how to actually begin. One of the women in my Aglow chapter began going in with another woman who had been teaching a weekly Bible study there for years. And through a strange turn of events, the chaplain called me one day and offered Aglow the opportunity to conduct monthly services for the women.

In January, 1988, Shortly after these monthly services had started, the chaplain asked me if we would be willing to take a weekly Bible study slot. The only problem was that he wanted a different person doing the teaching every week. This posed a serious problem for me, as I didn't see how our local chapter could persuade enough women to help with this. So I contacted the Area Board and asked if they could help us recruit women from all the chapters in the area in order to meet the chaplain's requirements. Since at that time I was personally preparing for a summer move back to Nairobi, Kenya, I gave the entire oversight of this jail ministry to the Area Board.

In the months before our return to Kenya for a three-year tour, I was experiencing a lot of pressure from many things. Physically, I was going through pre-menopause. Because of excessive bleeding I went through a D & C, although the doctor was recommending a hysterectomy. (I knew there was no way I could undergo major surgery and still be able to make preparations to move back to Kenya.) He told me the D & C would probably be good for only about three months, but I figured God could overrule that. At the very least, the D & C would buy me time to get the move accomplished.

Then, immediately after the D & C, my second grand-son was born in Augusta, Georgia. I went down to help my daughter-in-law even though I was myself physically exhausted. But while I was there, God's strength supernaturally permeated my being, His grace enabling me to do all that was needed for their family. The very moment we left there, God withdrew His anointing of strength, and I was totally overcome again by exhaustion.

I was facing what seemed an overwhelming task. We had lived in Virginia for eight years — the longest we had ever lived anywhere at one consecutive stretch. So we had accumulated lots of "stuff" we needed to sort through. Our shipment would be limited, so we had to figure out what to take with us, what to put into storage, and what to get rid of. We also had to sell two cars and buy one new one that the mechanics in Kenya would be capable of repairing, if necessary. We had to prepare the house for rental and find someone to move in. We had to have thorough physical exams for all of us at the Department of State, get the appropriate immunizations and new passports, and fill out paperwork galore.

I felt intense emotional pressure to resign from the Aglow presidency in order to accomplish all these things. But God would not allow me to release this responsibility until the last moment. I won't go into details about the reasons for this, only to say I myself did not fully understand them until after the fact. Then it became clear.

I also felt very strongly, in the depth of my heart, that Kenya was in for some serious turmoil, perhaps even a civil war. I even felt I may face martyrdom in my service for Jesus there. But I was fully resigned to that possibility. One of my Aglow sisters on my board also sensed that I would be in danger for my life, and she was struggling intensely with her feelings about this because she loved me dearly. I told her she would have to release me into God's hands. It was a very difficult time emotionally.

CHAPTER SEVEN

Challenges and Great Rewards

Upon our arrival in Nairobi, Kenya, the Embassy put us in temporary housing that was at the end of a badly washed out road and very isolated. We were very disappointed by the drastic changes in the city we had known before. The fact that the city workers had been on strike for a lengthy period prior to our arrival exacerbated the impact of the changes. Piles of rubbish were dumped all over the place! Buildings were rapidly going up everywhere, and the mud from the construction sites was washing into the roads and streets. The roads were more potholes than pavement! This formerly beautiful city was dirty, dusty, and ugly.

We began attending the International Christian Center — an A/G church where the pastors were a missionary couple from America and the people in the congregation were from more than a hundred nations. Shortly after we arrived there, we received a phone call with some disconcerting news from Chris, Mark's wife, back in the States. Immediately thereafter, our telephone went out and stayed out for over three weeks. And so we were left with no way to communicate with him and no way for me to talk to the pastor or his wife. There was nothing I could do to help him with his situation and I felt utterly helpless. All I could do was pray. Of course, that's always the most effective thing anyone can do in a crisis, anyway. And I can only say God took care of it.

Meanwhile, I felt increasingly frustrated. In addition to this, my hormonal imbalances were causing me to have absolutely no control over my emotions. The slightest thing would cause me to burst into tears. My brain told me it was utterly stupid, but I couldn't seem to help myself. Though I often felt alone and abandoned, God was with me and His grace saw me through.

We finally got settled in our assigned house. It was more easily accessible because it was on a paved road, but had serious challenges in many ways. The house was beautiful, and its architecture was unique. It was sitting on a hill over-looking the road. But it was in full sun all day. And it was built of materials that absorbed the heat of the sun during the day and radiated it into the rooms like an oven at night. So when the hot outdoor air would begin to cool off to a comfortable level in the evening, the indoor temperature kept climbing. The windows were situated in such a way that no breeze could get through the house. And the power lines would not support an air conditioner to help make things more bearable. This made for miserable sleeping conditions.

Not only that, but the water supply was also a constant problem. The amount of water would dwindle during the dry season, and the pressure was so low the water couldn't make it up the hill during the day because gardeners all along the road would be using it before it reached our house. When water did manage to get to the house during the early afternoon, it was only a trickle and looked very dirty. It turned out to be heavy with iron, making my clothes more and more dingy. We had a water storage tank in the attic to collect water during the night hours and we drew off of that during the days. But this made it difficult to wash clothes. Even when we were careful in our use of the water, it would frequently run out by the time we got to the dishes after dinner in the evenings. We were thrilled to be allowed to move to a new house in a year when the lease on this one expired!

My physical problems resumed by the end of that first summer. By October, on the recommendation of a local gynecologist, and at the insistence of our embassy doctor, I was on my way back to the States for a hysterectomy. Some friends, Sue and Charles Young, kindly opened their home to me to stay with them before and after the surgery, until I would be released by the doctor to return to my family in Kenya. This convalescent time was extremely difficult for me, away from my husband and youngest son. I had to really press in to the Lord to keep from wallowing in self-pity.

When I finally got back after about seven weeks away, I found things not going very well in our household. Although I had found a friend in the wife of our pastor, at just the time when I needed her support the most, she had to return to the States for an extended stay with her kids. God was teaching me that I needed to lean on Him alone, not any human friend, no matter how close.

Some time after our move to Nairobi, I shared with some local spiritual leaders what I had sensed God was saying about Kenya's future, and they confirmed that God had been speaking the same thing to them. We agreed this was a warning to pray and intercede for Kenya. Perhaps God would spare the nation. (As it turned out, toward the end of our three-year tour, there were indeed some serious problems that brought widespread bloody rioting, with many lives lost, for a lengthy period of time. But God spared us, and in some cases He protected our missionaries in a supernatural way from imminent danger.)

While I was living in Nairobi, the opportunities for ministry were very slow in developing. My first opportunity outside my church came through a young minister named Habil who was busy starting churches all over the place. He invited me to come on a Sunday after lunch and speak to a church in the slums, in a part of Nairobi called Kibera. I was told there were 750,000 people living in this slum. Had we known beforehand what this place was like, my husband John would never have allowed me to go. But God carried me the whole time and I had no fear whatsoever, but was filled with joy and a strange peace.

Habil told me where to park, in a place where my car would hopefully be safe from thieves and vandals, although he didn't explain that to me beforehand. He had someone meet me and walk me through to the very center of the slums where there was an open space of barren dirt, totally devoid of grass, with a small tin building. This was the YMCA building. Kids were playing soccer in the dirt field around it. They had a fire going outside with a huge pot on it, in which some of the women were cooking lunch for everyone in the church. I had been asked to come and speak at 1:00 P.M. This young minister had already been preaching all morning. After they broke for lunch, he continued preaching. He finally let me speak at about 4:00 P.M.! Then he resumed preaching as the escort walked me back out of the place and to my car. I was utterly amazed at the spiritual hunger in the hearts of these people to cause them to endure this lengthy meeting.

Later on, Habil took me with him to speak at a girls' school in another town outside Nairobi. Because of this speaking engagement in this school, I later received two other invitations from these girls to preach in their meetings during our stay in Nairobi. This was a very interesting situation. The school was a Catholic boarding school, where the girls lived for three months at a time, returning to their farm-houses for a month in between their quarterly scholastic sessions. On this school campus was a group of young Protestant girls who ran a church service on Sunday mornings to which they would invite outside speakers to come and preach. They had their own choir and led their own service. They even made their own decisions about whom to invite and served them refreshments afterward! What a thrill to be asked to minister to this group of "on-fire" young ladies! We saw several girls receive Christ every time I was there.

On my third and last invitation to speak to these girls, my husband came along. He and I marveled at their freedom and zeal to carry on their own worship services in this situation! We both sadly acknowledged how impossible this would be in America today!

Another time, I received an invitation to speak to the Women's Aglow there in Nairobi. They were quite a blessing. Imagine a local Aglow meeting with close to 1000 women in attendance! Back in the States, our local meetings were considered to have done well if they managed to get 60 or more women to attend. What a great privilege it was for me to share the Word of God with them.

The pastor in our International Christian Church allowed me to preach several times. I had been asked to teach a series on love in the Adult Sunday school class just before I left for my lengthy medical stay back in Virginia. After my return to Nairobi, I began teaching this Adult Sunday school class regularly. I believe that played a part in getting invitations to speak at other places.

A woman who sometimes attended our church came to the Sunday school class I was teaching. She was used of God to open a number of other doors in churches and organizations for me to speak. I spoke to the women's group at the All Saints (Anglican) Cathedral in the heart of Nairobi twice, and to the entire church once during a special 3-day week-end event. The wife of one of the Cabinet officers in Kenya's government attended one of those women's meetings. Someone who heard me there got me invited to a Presbyterian church to speak to their women. Somehow I later got an invitation to speak to a group of couples at an AME church. I had an opportunity to share my testimony in the Christian Women's Club of Nairobi. I was told afterward that they had more women sign the pledge card (saying that they had prayed with me for salvation) than they had ever had before! I could only praise God for this blessing, for it was His doing! It was awesome to see how God began opening doors in almost a chain-reaction fashion.

Another woman who attended our church had her own devotional radio program on a worldwide shortwave radio station called Trans World Radio Africa. Although she prepared her program at a studio in Nairobi, the tapes would be sent to South Africa where the messages would then be broadcast all over Africa and the Indian Ocean areas. She invited me to be a guest speaker for her program and to prepare five consecutive short devotions, which were then sent to South Africa for broadcasting. I understood that the program would probably be sent on from there to Guam, where it would be broadcast all over the Pacific! Only God would know what the impact could be on how many people!

My pastors asked me to do counseling in some particularly difficult situations, and they would first take me to meet the people they wanted me to minister to. One was actually being beaten by her husband when we arrived on the scene, a common practice in Kenyan society! Another lovely Indian girl was in need of much encouragement, as she had physical challenges that caused her to feel very much an outcast. She was dating a wonderful Christian young man. Both of them were facing active persecution from their Hindu families. I had the privilege of spending a lot of time with them both and ended up giving them pre-marriage counseling. They were married and had a baby girl before we left Kenya. This couple is currently living in Texas with their lovely little girl!

Another woman and her husband had a situation which was especially heartbreaking. This couple already had a beautiful little girl when she became pregnant with a boy. Sons are very important to Kenyan men. Although she had previously given birth by cesarian section, she wanted to have this baby by natural birth. The doctor felt it was a good possibility she could do that. Unfortunately, while she was in labor she was not being closely monitored. The result was that her uterus ruptured and, before she could get help, she lost not only the baby she was carrying but her uterus as well. It was a miracle she didn't lose her own life!

This hysterectomy was a severe blow to her since it meant she had lost her ability to ever have more children of her own. In Kenyan society, the ability to give a man a son is the primary, if not the only, source of a woman's self-worth. Not only had she lost a precious life she had been anticipating for nine months, and thus was enveloped in unbearable grief, but she was also grieving the loss of a future and all her sense of self-worth. Her anger toward the doctor and all the other medical personnel was overwhelming but understandable.

By the time I left Kenya to return to the States, she was better able to deal with the anger and grief. She and her husband gave me (typical for this part of the world) a parting gift — two live chickens! This was a few days before our departure for America, and all of our belongings except for our clothes and suitcases had already been packed and shipped out. Needless to say, these two chickens ended up with some missionary friends who already had some chickens in their menagerie of many different animals.

While in Kenya, I had gone on a few outings to speak in various women's meetings in outlying A/G churches with some of the missionaries. And now and then I would have the opportunity to preach in my own church, where our family worshiped regularly. But I longed for opportunities to preach in other A/G churches of Kenya, since my ministerial credentials were with the Assemblies of God. But no one seemed to know I was there.

It seems that God is forever teaching me patience, which I greatly need, because I have always been a very impatient person. I can't tell you how many times, when I would be earnestly seeking God to open doors for me, He would say "wait." I seemed to stay in limbo for years, as I waited for God to say "Now you're ready to go preach the Gospel." Also, it seemed to me that every time the doors started to open for me to teach or otherwise serve the Lord, we would be transferred elsewhere, and I had to start all over. Every time I tried in my own way to get doors opened, something would happen to slam them shut.

One time I was all set to meet the Kenyan General Superintendent of the A/G. I believe I was told by one of the missionaries, and I believed it, that meeting him would be a key to getting doors opened to preach in the other A/G churches there. But on the morning I was going to go with a missionary friend to meet him, I woke up violently dizzy, and the slightest motion would cause my stomach to start heaving.

This led to several weeks of being totally incapacitated, because any movement on my part set the room spinning and my stomach heaving. The official diagnosis by our embassy physician (after several weeks of visits, while he was out of the country, to all sorts of Nairobi specialists to rule out brain tumors or other more exotic ailments) was labyrinthitis, an inflammation of the inner ear. It took a few months to get better to the point I could drive again. And there are still, to this day, some vague, lingering effects from this problem which affects my sense of balance. Needless to say, I felt very frustrated by my physical inability to do what I had wanted so much to do. But God has quite a sense of humor. You'll see what I mean in this next story.

After my equilibrium recovered sufficiently for me to travel, an A/G missionary friend named Marilyn invited me to go with her on a week's journey out to a district in the area of Kenya that bordered on Uganda. We drove a day's journey from Nairobi, to a centralized town where we checked into our "headquarters" hotel. From there we traveled to a different sectional meeting each day to address the women. Marilyn would teach first and then I would preach. We gave the same messages at each meeting so that each group of women received the same teaching and preaching.

It just so happened that the Kenyan General Superintendent, whom I had been trying unsuccessfully to meet at the time I developed the inner ear problem, was going to be meeting with the pastors and elders of all the churches in each section at the same time and place where we were going to be ministering to the women!

This preaching trip was an exciting adventure! These little churches were out in the middle of nowhere and thus difficult to reach. We had to travel on unpaved dirt highways and roads. The dust, as fine as talcum powder, infiltrated every crack of the vehicle, and settled all over us and our belongings. The last bit of the way to several of the churches involved driving through fields and along footpaths. I was constantly amazed at how well the missionary's small European car handled as we traveled where there were no roads, even over washed-out areas. Marilyn seemed daring and fearless in her driving!

The church buildings were generally small, and all except one of the five churches we visited were constructed like the peoples' huts in this area. The walls of the buildings were created by making a mesh framework of small tree limbs and sticks of varying sizes and then packing the spaces with a plaster made from dirt, cow dung, and water. The stench could be really overpowering, especially when the "plaster" was new! The buildings were packed with 100-350 people who had walked many miles to reach the meeting and who would sleep on the floors or the ground outdoors.

On the first morning out, the church building where we met was completely exposed to the sun out in a field, with several small huts of the pastor and his family nearby. It was only about 20 feet wide and maybe 45 feet long, with nothing but dirt for a floor. The roof was made of thatched grass. The only seats were a few benches consisting of a single rough board about 1 X 6 on some blocks. (I found this same sort of seating in a number of places where I had the privilege of preaching in the outer areas of Kenya. Inside Nairobi all the churches, except the two I visited which were in the slums, had regular chairs or pews.)

Anyway, this building was packed full of people, wall-to-wall, who were sitting on the dirt floor or standing where they could hear the messages. Marilyn and I were up front. Fortunately, I was right next to a side door, because the smell was making my stomach very queasy. I didn't understand anything that was being said the whole day because everything was in Swahili. My message was going to be preached in English and translated into Swahili. The women were inside the church for the first part of the day, and the men met outside, under some trees.

Just before it was my turn to speak, about 11:00 A.M., I found out that the General Superintendent had decided he wanted me to speak to the men as well as the women! It seems he wanted to hear me preach! (See what I meant by the statement that God has a sense of humor?!!) This necessitated a shift in the time I would speak, because he wouldn't be done with the men by the time I was scheduled to preach to the women. And a serious problem was that I had prepared a message of encouragement particularly for women, based on the story of Hannah, mother of Samuel.

I got up and stepped outside, feeling really nauseated by

the smell, the stifling heat, and the anxiety of preaching to the pastors and the General Superintendent a message which had been designed specifically for women! Not only did I need the fresh air, but I needed time to collect my thoughts and pray about how to amend my message to make it applicable to men as well as women. I confess I didn't know exactly how I was going to do that, but I knew God can do anything, so I asked Him to help me, as I preached, to find the application for these men as well. And praise God, He did!

Home life, particularly family relationships, in Kenya was very similar to that of the Jews in the days of Hannah. Issues of childbearing, sons to carry on the heritage, the way men treated women, polygamy, and jealousy between plural wives were current problems in the homes of Kenya. So this message about Hannah, a woman who was being tormented by her jealous co-wife because she was barren, was very relevant to the people of Kenya.

When I finished the message, the Kenyan General Superintendent got up and addressed the men — pastors of local churches — and shared his own testimony of how the things I preached applied to him! The personal things he shared were things most men would never share with others in the Kenyan society! A man would not usually talk publicly about emotional or personal issues! After he finished speaking, he left the meeting and went on to the host pastor's house to start on his lunch. He sent word back asking me to join him there.

I was very surprised by this turn of events. As he and I sat down to the V.I.P. lunch prepared especially for the leaders of the meetings, I felt a little apprehensive, not knowing what to expect. (Not to mention, it was extremely hard to ignore the fly swimming in the chicken soup! But I had to be polite.) It seems that almost every day of our five days in that area we were served the same meal — boiled chicken, rice, and ugali. Ugali is a mush of ground corn boiled in water, similar to the grits eaten in the southern United States, but much thicker and stickier so it could be eaten with the hands. I got very tired of the V.I.P. lunch and was literally sick with galloping diarrhea and nausea before our week was over!

But what the Superintendent especially wanted to tell me, as we sat together in this pastor's home, was that he wanted me to preach that same message to all of the pastors at each of the next four meetings we had set up. He also said he wanted me to preach it in every A/G church in Kenya! (That didn't happen, due to the short time I had left before we would return to America.) And he wanted me to preach it in his own church in Nairobi. (I did get to do that!) He had the largest Assembly of God church in the country.

On the third day of this trip I began to feel vague intestinal rumblings and slight nausea. By the fourth day I was running to the outhouse every few minutes! I was desperately praying for God to touch me and enable me to preach. When it came time for me to get up and preach, and for the entire time (an hour or so) while I was preaching and it was being interpreted, I felt just fine. But the moment I sat back down the diarrhea would hit again!

I've often wondered why God didn't take the problem totally away. Obviously He could have healed me completely, but He chose to just relieve the problem while I preached. I now believe it was because He wanted me to remain totally dependent on Him the entire time and to know it was <u>He</u>, and not I, who enabled me to preach. This taught me the truth of the following Scriptures: *"Let us then approach the throne of grace with confidence, so that we may receive mercy and find grace to help us **in our time of need.**"* (Heb. 4:16) *"But he said to me, '**My grace is sufficient for you**, for my power is made perfect in weakness.' Therefore I will boast all the more gladly about my weaknesses, so that Christ's power may rest* *on me."* (2 Corinthians 12:9)

The last meeting day of our week-long trip was in a brand-new church. The stench of this newly "plastered" building was unbelievable! By now I was not only running every 10-15 minutes to the hole in the ground that served as an outhouse, but feeling very sick to my stomach. I thought, after the service, that there was no way I could eat any of the V.I.P. lunch. But my friend reminded me it would be a serious breach of protocol, and offensive to the hosts, if I failed to eat something. But it seemed this was the greasiest of all the V.I.P. lunches! After a few bites I managed to excuse myself, with my missionary friend explaining how ill I was. I prayed I would get back to our hotel headquarters without vomiting. Thank God He answered that prayer.

Then there came an extremely serious question: how in the world could I make it back to Nairobi the next day? This was a full day's drive, with no rest stops, no gas stations with restrooms, no restaurants with restrooms, no place along the way to stop. I prayed earnestly for God to help me in this situation too! And God heard and answered my pleas, by stopping my diarrhea until I got back home to Nairobi. It returned the day after I got home, but at least there I could receive medical treatment. God certainly taught me all through this trip that His grace is sufficient for me in the time of need!

A week or so later we traveled to another town where we were to spend two nights, ministering at a church in that town. Then we were to drive to another town to spend the night and minister at another church on our way back home. However, my stomach problems returned that first morning out, and I was unable to help Marilyn at the first church. But I stayed in our hotel room and prayed for her. It turned out that she was in much need of prayer as she had to deal with a serious problem between some of the leaders. Thankfully, after taking some medication, I was able to assist her at the next church.

Once, I had the privilege of ministering to the women of an A/G church that was in the process of constructing a beautiful new block building right in the middle of the largest slum in Nairobi. I was told that this slum, in Muthare Valley, had a million people living in it! There was an insane asylum up the hill. The living conditions were unbelievable. Open ditches carried sewage right past people's front doors and, in many places, even through their huts. We had to criss-cross one of these ditches as we wove our way toward the meeting place.

The dwellings were made of cardboard boxes and scraps of wood or metal or whatever could be put to use to provide shelter. They would have only a foot to five feet between dwellings. The stench was terrible, and the conditions so dangerous that a whole group of people had to surround me and my missionary friend to escort us in from our parking area to this meeting. Our escorts had told us to give them our purses to carry, and to take off any jewelry, including our watches, so they couldn't be grabbed or ripped off of us along the way. The thugs lining the path were muttering in Swahili about how we had removed our watches! Had I realized at the time what they were saying, it probably would have produced fear in my heart.

The women sat in the church with their backs to a wall made of rough boards with big gaps. Right behind this "wall" was a cement mixer that was running to provide cement for the construction! It made it very difficult for them to hear me over the noise, and my voice was almost gone from all the preaching I had been doing. I was totally blown out of the water by the hospitality of this little group. They wanted to provide us with refreshments, but had nothing to cook with. So they gave us about three dozen raw eggs to take home.

I felt really bad about taking it from people who had so little, but I couldn't insult them. I was in awe that those who had so little gave us something of great value and cost to them! Only one other group I had spoken to in all my time in Kenya had given me any kind of gift for speaking! And they gave me a towel, one of some specially decorated ones they were selling for a fund-raiser!

Shortly after this, my friend Marilyn invited me to go with her on a one-day outing to a little church a couple of hours away from Nairobi. The road was notoriously bad, and Marilyn's husband Glenn, being very worried about the possibility of our being stuck on a road to such a dangerous place, sternly warned her to turn around and not continue on to the meeting if the road seemed bad. The church itself was on a mountain in a place known as Hell's Gate. It was a very dangerous place for any woman, let alone two white women, to be stuck at night. We had three Kenyan women in the back seat, one of whom was the national leader of the Women's Ministries for the Kenyan Assemblies of God. The other two were from this area and were supposed to be guiding us to the church, which even my missionary friend Marilyn had never seen.

As we left the paved road, we soon came to an unbelievable stretch of powdery, rutted sand, about six to eight inches deep, which appeared to be about 600 yards or more in length and covered the entire width of the unpaved road, about 25 or 30 feet! Marilyn stopped the car and got out to check out the situation. It was finely powdered lava, about the consistency of talcum powder. While we sat there in this stuff, trying to decide whether to go on or turn back, we were passed by a matatu.

Matatus were the local equivalent of a bus. It usually was a pick-up truck or van turned into a bus-like apparatus which the people crammed into with their baggage piled on top. Many times the people would be hanging out the back door or out the windows. We thought if that matatu could get through this bad stretch, surely we could, also. And our passengers assured us that our destination wasn't very much further, and that there were only one or two other bad areas (and they were supposedly not as bad as this) on the route.

So we began praying in the Spirit and headed through it. Surprisingly, the little car seemed to make it through without too much trouble. Before long we came to another patch of equal size. With much prayer we made it through that one. Then we came to a patch that was even worse. The road actually had some areas that had been washed out, leaving a "cliff" facing us about two to four feet high! (Remember this for later.) But off to the side was an area where people had been driving, making another road to go around the washed-out area. So we took that route and made it through!

At each bad stretch the women in the back would plead with us not to turn back, assuring us that it was only a little further, and that there weren't more than one or two bad spots the rest of the way. They appealed to us not to let the women down who had traveled for many miles to get to the meeting!

Unfortunately, the Kenyan people who don't drive had no concept of distance. We drove for many, many more miles before we finally arrived at the little path leading up the mountain to the church! And at the very moment Marilyn pulled off the dirt road into that path, the car quit running! As she tried unsuccessfully to re-start the car, she had a sinking feeling, accompanied by a growing anger that she had failed to turn around at the first or second bad area and return to Nairobi! Here we were, stranded in the middle of nowhere, in a very dangerous part of Kenya, with no help to be seen. The odds of finding help in this remote area were very slim. And the nearest telephone was many miles back in the last town where the road was still paved! So there was no way to call anyone for help.

In Kenya, it seemed that everyone thought he was a fine mechanic. Unfortunately, they could ruin your car if you let them mess with it. We had been warned by the Embassy not to ever allow a passerby to work on our car if it broke down!

Marilyn asked the pastor of the church if there was a mechanic in the town. (The "town" was so small there were only a few buildings and houses.) He answered that he didn't know! He sent someone to inquire for us and, sure enough, someone showed up. I thought the problem with the car was caused by all that fine dust and dirt that were no doubt clogging the air intake of the carburetor. But he went straight to the points. Somehow, miraculously, after a lengthy period of time, he got the car running. I can't help wondering if he was an angel sent from God to our rescue.

At some point during this ordeal, we had gone on up the mountain on foot (it was only wide enough to walk up anyway, the ledge being too narrow for a car). The local women hoisted all our supplies onto their heads to carry them up the mountain. I can't begin to describe the beauty of the spot. This little church was perched on a mountain from which you could see for probably 100 miles in all but one direction! It was built of rough-hewn boards with gaping spaces between them. The inside was covered with pieces of cardboard boxes to try to slow down the wind that would howl through the building much of the time. The dirt floor was covered with straw.

My heart was broken at the time over something that was going on with my youngest son, away at college in Virginia at this very time. And my broken-ness spilled over in compassion for these women. As the invitation was given, they crowded to the front and began to pour out their hearts to God. Tears were streaming down their faces as they communed with our Savior.

After the meeting Marilyn decided to forego lunch with the pastor in order to try to get back to civilization where she could get help if the car broke down again. We packed our stuff and headed back, fully conscious of the precarious situation we were in. We left the two local women behind, so there were only Marilyn, the Kenyan leader of women's ministries, and I. We prayed in the Spirit the entire way back to the paved highway! The car literally flew over that two-to-four foot drop-off of washed-out road (I told you earlier to remember this one), landed with only a mild plop, and continued through the fine powdered "sand" without stopping! I felt like the angels were carrying us all the way. When we got near the little town where the roads were paved, the car started missing. Marilyn headed to the town to try to get to a telephone. She got to the middle of town when the car died again!

In answer to our prayers, Marilyn was able to find a telephone that actually worked (often a miracle in itself in Kenya!) and got hold of her husband in Nairobi. She told Glenn about the previous problem and how the man had gotten the car going again by cleaning the points, and he came to our rescue, bringing a new set of points with him. It took him a couple of hours to arrive at this little town. He is an excellent mechanic himself and got the car running again. But, as it turned out, our dangerous trip was not over.

We had barely gotten off the side road onto the main highway, heading up over the Escarpment from the Rift Valley toward Nairobi, when the car stopped again. We coasted off the road, honking the horn, and Glenn stopped to check out our car. Smoke was coming from some of the wiring in the engine compartment! He discovered that the wires to the ignition system had shorted out. He got a short rope from his car, connected it to his car bumper, and headed up the steep mountainous terrain, pulling our car with his.

As we began ascending higher and higher, the rope began slipping off the bumper of his car. We honked the horn and got him to stop. When he got the rope repositioned on something more solid and tried to start moving up the incline with our car in tow, it started to rip the bumper loose.

Again, we honked and he slammed on his brakes. Marilyn also put on her brakes so we wouldn't roll back down the mountain. He decided he would try to let our car roll backwards and maneuver it as far as possible off the road (though there was no shoulder to speak of). He would then drive us on in his car to where we could get help. At this point, he discovered that his car would not move at all because the brakes had gotten so hot they locked up. So here we were on the very steep incline of the mountain, and our car's motor wouldn't run and his car couldn't move! And by this time darkness had closed in.

Now, in these mountains of Kenya this is an extremely dangerous position to be in! If you get stranded on the road, you're a sitting target for the roaming bandits who are likely to either shoot you or cut off your head with a machete and rob you. But there is another danger that makes it imperative to get out of your car — some vehicle loaded with people may come along and slam into your car and kill you and themselves! But we had no place to go because there was barely any shoulder on the road to move our car onto, and his was stuck in the middle of the road because of the frozen brakes!

As Glenn got into our car and began trying to figure out a way to get it to run, we were praying big-time! I was asking God to give him wisdom on how to fix the car. Suddenly one of us had an inspiration! Maybe he could pull a wire from the radio to replace the burned out one! That's exactly what he did. Then he was able to get our car started. Since there was no way we could move his car, we had to leave it there and pray no one would hit it before we could send someone back to pick it up and remove it from the road.

All of us piled into Marilyn's jury-rigged car and headed up and over the mountain. Glenn thought there was a pastor's house just on the other side of the mountain. As it turned out, it was at least 15 minutes of very fast driving, up and down and around the mountains, with Glenn and Marilyn worried sick that someone would hit his abandoned car and get killed!

When we arrived at the pastor's house, Glenn and several men went back in another vehicle to see if they could physically pick up his car and remove it from the road. But when they got there the brakes had already cooled down and were no longer locked. He was able to drive it on to the pastor's house where he picked up Marilyn and me and we headed back to Nairobi, leaving Marilyn's damaged car at the pastor's house to be fixed and picked up later.

I was amazingly calm throughout this entire trip. In fact, I marveled at the peace I was walking in, even as it happened! I can only attribute this to one thing. I was being carried by the arms of Jesus. Of course, others could say it was because I was too ignorant of the dangers at the time, which may have been true. But I know that my trust was in Jesus, and we were on His business that day!

We were very grateful to have made it home alive and well from that trip, although it was hours later than the time we were supposed to be home! We were all dirty and tired and hungry. Then Glenn had to go back a few days later and work on Marilyn's car in order to drive it home. It needed a total overhaul after that trip, with many parts in the engine having to be replaced! And when he thought it was well enough to travel again, we planned another one-day trip, only to have to cancel it when the car started missing again!

I don't know how long it took Marilyn to be able to forgive herself for disregarding her husband's warning to turn around if the road got bad, but God saw us safely home anyway. Praise the Lord!

While we had thoroughly enjoyed our first two tours in Nairobi between 1976-1980, John had a very difficult time emotionally all the way through this last tour, from 1988 to1991. He had been greatly disappointed because things had so drastically changed for the worse in Nairobi during the eight years we had been back in the States. Also, John had grown to love our Virginia house and yard, and the comforts of living in the States — especially watching football games on TV — so he found himself more and more homesick to return.

But by the time we got our orders to leave, I wished very much I could stay in Kenya to take advantage of the wonderful opportunities that had just begun to open for me to minister for the Lord. It was exceedingly difficult and heart-rending for me to leave just when so many more doors were beginning to open for me to preach and teach the Word of God! My heart was still in Kenya for several years after our return to the States, until one day the Lord spoke to my heart during a prayer meeting and showed me very clearly that the Washington, D.C. area was also very much a foreign mission field.

CHAPTER EIGHT

New Directions

Wherever God allowed me to minister in Kenya, I always marveled at the faith and sincerity of the people. Their worship was without any of our familiar instruments, as they had only rudimentary, homemade instruments, such as drums or triangles with a nail to strike for sound. But their singing was with such harmony I thought I had been transported to heaven itself. Even though I knew none of the words they were singing in Swahili, in my spirit I was able to worship along with them. I never felt out of place, even when I was the only white person there. This is God's amazing grace!

When the preaching was finished and an altar call given, they would flock to the front and cry out with many tears to the Lord. They had very open and tender hearts toward God. What a glorious move of the Holy Spirit I witnessed, over and over again, in this land where the people had few possessions but were hungry for God. We in America could learn a lot from our brothers and sisters in other countries because we are so caught up in greed and materialism. We too often find our satisfaction and contentment in our possessions rather than in God! Materialism is idolatry — what God calls spiritual adultery! I was greatly disappointed after I returned to the States because of the complacency and indifference I found in the Christians here. It was such a contrast with the hunger I had witnessed among the people of Kenya.

During my time in Kenya, I took many Bible school and university courses to qualify for the "Christian Worker" and "License to Preach" credentials with the Assemblies of God. It took me less than a year after arriving there to qualify for the first, entry-level credentials. On my first home leave, in the summer of 1989, I met with the District credentials committee.

When we arrived back in Kenya, I was shocked to find mail from the District addressed to me as "Rev. Margaret Wolf." Being from a Baptist background, where you have people "licensed" to preach (with little preparation or requirements), and only the "ordained" ministers can pastor a church, I had no idea that a "Christian Worker" was granted that title, and was considered to be qualified to pastor a church! (Though I had wondered why the requirements were so stringent for such a simple title!) They have since changed the name of this credential to "Certified Minister."

As we approached the time to return to the States, I began thinking and praying about where God might have me serve Him there. I had studied two more years and gotten much more experience in ministry to qualify for the second level, or "License to Preach," credentials by the time we left Kenya. At that point I was thinking perhaps I should start out in some place as an associate pastor to learn the ropes of how to be a pastor. But one thing I know is the fact that I can never figure out what God has in store for me. I always try to, but just when I think I know what His plans are, He usually surprises me. And this time, also, it seemed God had different plans.

After my return to Virginia, in the summer of 1991, I met again with the Potomac District credentials committee and then received my new credentials. As I began looking around at possible openings in churches, the Women's Aglow Area Board covering northern Virginia asked me if I would take over as the chairwoman of the jail ministry, which at that point ministered in only one jail, the Fairfax County Adult Detention Center (ADC). Although I wanted to go back into the jail to preach and minister to the women there, I didn't want to be the one in charge of that ministry! But God showed me within a few months that this was His plan for me!

At about the same time that I said "yes" to the Area Board in the fall of 1991, Aglow's weekly jail Bible Study was closed by the chaplain, so we had only the monthly church service to conduct, every third Sunday. But in January, 1992, the chaplain offered me a brand new slot for a weekly Bible Study. This was an answer to prayer and fulfillment of a prophetic word God had spoken to me, so I jumped at the chance.

This Bible Study became a major school of the Holy Spirit for me. Over the weeks and months, as I went every week to minister to these women, God taught me how to move more and more freely in His Spirit. At the beginning, I felt I had to be fully prepared with a well-developed message. But usually God took over and I hardly used my notes. Then it got more and more difficult to even know ahead of time what He wanted me to teach. It seemed when I had a pre-planned message God would change it on me before I could deliver it! I was learning more and more how to trust Him to use me as His instrument to deliver the message He desired, even when it wasn't what I expected it to be. I truly learned how to open my mouth and let Him fill it with His Word.

I'm not advocating that anyone should ever fail to be

prepared. But I am saying "Don't leave God out and try to do it all yourself!" My own personal tendencies have been to lean too much on myself — my knowledge, my research, my understanding, my plans. God was breaking me of that dependence on myself and teaching me to rely on His Holy Spirit so I would know that He is able to work through me. Now, if God is gracious enough to give me directions as to the message ahead of time, or if I just have a "leading" to teach a certain topic, I will do whatever research I can and then speak whatever God brings out of my mouth.

What a wonderful thrill to be a part of what God was doing in the jail! These women were not just a captive audience. They were hungry for God and His Word. They were often discouraged and downhearted. But God moved over and over again to touch their hearts and lives, to change their attitudes and desires. The women who went in with me and I could see the difference in their faces when God touched them. We could rejoice with them when prayers were answered. We were thrilled to see some of these women becoming active in ministering to one another in their cell blocks where we ourselves couldn't go. We saw many lives brought to the Lord over the years, and many souls brought back after backsliding. Some of them have been successfully rehabilitated and we know God is continuing to work in their lives on the outside.

Initially, I was also ministering one-on-one to some of the women. The chaplain's office would select a woman for me to mentor, and I would visit her in the same small rooms where inmates would visit with their lawyers. I would arrange with her which day and time and then go weekly to personally teach and pray with and minister to her.

One woman whom I mentored for several months was a very difficult case. I found myself seriously struggling and earnestly praying for wisdom and for God to give me a breakthrough with her. Finally the truth came out, showing me the real nature of the problem. Her father had sexually molested her as a child, and she was a practicing homosexual. This sin is a serious problem in jail. I planted much seed of God's Word in her but didn't see much fruit before she was transferred to another jail, away from my influence.

The jail ministry is very rewarding but can also be very difficult. Because of the demonic activity in the lives of so many inmates (not to mention some of the deputies), we were waging a real war for the souls of these women.

I constantly asked people to pray for protection for the women going in to the jail to preach or teach, as well as for God's anointing to come upon and break the yoke off the inmates as the women ministered. It's imperative that those who go into the jail to minister be covered by intercessors' prayers.

About a year after I took over as jail ministry chairwoman, I was asked to join the Northern Virginia Area Board of Aglow International in the position of Vice President of Ministries. Because I had already been prepared by the Lord for this ministry, I readily accepted the call. I asked a dear friend whom God had already prepared for this, to take over the leadership of this weekly Bible study in the jail. I continued to serve as jail ministry chairwoman for the entire time I was on the Area Board except for one year, and also remained available to fill in to teach the class or help in those times when I would be needed. I still go in and preach in the jail at least once a month.

The ADC has also been a place where I was blessed more than the women to whom I ministered. Every person who went into the jail for this ministry said the same thing. I would often ask God, before I went in to preach, to give me one or more souls that day. And most days we had at least one woman receive Jesus as her Savior. Many times we would experience a powerful move of God's Holy Spirit and these inmates would be weeping and pouring out their hearts to God. No matter what happened while we were there, it always lifted our spirits and caused us to go out rejoicing in God's goodness for what He did while we were in the jail!

In my family, during all these years, we have walked through many valleys. But the valleys are the places for much spiritual growth. Jesus said, *"In this world you will have trouble. But take heart! I have overcome the world"* (John 16:33). Jesus is our victory. This One who has already overcome the world walked with us through the difficult times as well as the good ones.

Our home life was in much transition right after our return from Kenya, as Bobby moved out of his apartment and into our basement. Although Bobby was engaged to be married, he needed some time to get on his feet financially and make preparations for a home of his own. He moved into a townhouse not far away when he married Cindy. Later, after their first child was born, they bought a house in Sterling, about a 40 minute drive from us.

Our youngest son, David, had been very strongly influenced in the wrong direction by a girl living in our compound while we were still in Kenya. This girl hated her mother and was constantly venting her anger and hatred to David, who was listen with growing sympathy. This was a time when I really saw the truth about "what goes in comes out," or as the computer people say, "garbage in, garbage out." Her attitudes toward her mother rubbed off on him and became his attitudes toward me. I could feel those angry, rebellious attitudes as they developed in David toward me.

When David came back to Virginia to start his first year of college, his rebellious attitude got him into serious difficulties and he ended up getting suspended from school and returning to Kenya for the remainder of our tour there. When we returned to the States and moved back into our house in Virginia, he was in a major depression.

Shortly after our return, he got seriously involved with a girl we didn't know. I had to have a difficult conversation with him in which I warned him that sin has its consequences, using the example of King David in the Bible. He didn't want to listen. But within a matter of a day or two, he ended up in the hospital with excruciating pain in every joint and muscle making it impossible for him to even move! During the three days he was there the doctors could find no reason for his problem, despite extensive tests.

While he was there, his girlfriend came by the house to pick up something he wanted her to bring him. I noticed she was wearing a pentagram on a chain around her neck. I pretended not to recognize it and asked about it. Her response was to the effect that she had been in a mainline church but didn't find what she was looking for there. So she began searching the old religions and found much more of what she was looking for. When she was finished and ready to leave, the Holy Spirit came upon me and I began to share with her my testimony and how exciting it is to have a real, living, vital relationship with the living God. For some reason she hastily broke up with David! She couldn't stand up to the Word of God, delivered in His love under the anointing of the Holy Spirit.

David was exceedingly angry about that turn of events. Interestingly, after he had taken up with still another girl (who claimed to be a Christian) I chastised him for getting into fornication with another girl after what he had gone through with the first one.

He said, "At least this girl isn't a witch."

I was taken by surprise and had to come back to him and ask, "Do you mean to tell me you <u>knew</u> she was a witch?"

He replied, "Yes, but I thought I could get away with having a relationship with her!"

This is a sad thing about many Christians today. They seem to think they can play with fire and not get burned.

Some even refuse to believe that the devil or evil spirits are active in our world today. They seem to think the Bible stories about demons were just superstitions or myths.

When David and the second girl got married in January, 1996, they moved into our basement. God gave both John and me a very similar warning dream on the same night, prior to their moving in with us! I dreamed I was surrounded by snakes in our back yard and I was killing them as fast as I could. John dreamed that there were snakes all over the place and he was telling me to kill them! For those who don't know it, snakes have always been symbolic of the devil or evil spirits. They literally brought a snake, Komodo dragon, iguana, and hamster with them.

On October 31, 1996, less than a year after David's marriage to this girl, my mother-in-law moved in with us also. We had quite a struggle finding ways to store items from three households! I am truly blessed to have an administrative husband who sees the overall picture and can organize things very well. It took him many months to get our unfinished portion of the basement into some kind of order where we could move around and still find things. Needless to say we had to get rid of a lot of stuff. Clashes between various personalities in this three-generational home created their own challenges and tensions. I'll have to say these challenges were opportunities either to grow spiritually or to backslide!

It seems David's bride was fascinated by dragons, lizards, and snakes, and she was also into Druids and who knows what else. She spent the entire time she lived here driving a wider and wider wedge between us and David. I watched with much grief as she seemed to become more and more involved romantically with another man. Fully persuaded that if I said anything to David he would not believe me and it would drive him further away, I could only pray. This was a very difficult situation until she left him and moved in with her boyfriend near the end of 1998. She moved out the very night of the afternoon when I had suddenly risen up under the anointing of the Holy Spirit, and said to the <u>devil</u>: "Satan, get out of here and leave my kids alone!"

When David's wife left him, he was heartbroken. He tried to get her to go to counseling with him, but she refused. Eventually he began coming out from under her spell. He found another wife over the internet (not a good idea!) and was happy for a while. Unfortunately he didn't really know her very well. He moved up to Maine to be near her family, because she said she couldn't leave them. David was her third husband, and she had some serious mental problems and was being treated for bipolar disorder, of which he was unaware. She, too, left him and moved out after about a year, filing for divorce as she moved in with her boss!

David's inlaws were very upset by this turn of events. They took him under their collective "wings" and nurtured him for a little over a year, when he sold his house in Maine and moved to Georgia, about five miles from his older brother Mark and his family. The Lord led Chris to just the right house for David to buy, and he's very happy there. He's also beginning his journey back to the Lord, attending the same church Mark and Chris attend.

After Bobby's second son (my fifth grandson) Christopher was born, we noticed he was having problems with his muscles, causing his hands and arms to jerk spasmodically. He seemed not to be developing properly in many ways. After many tests by many specialists, he was diagnosed as having microcephaly (abnormally small head), mild cerebral palsy, underdeveloped fine motor skills and overdeveloped major motor skills, and several developmental delays. My son called me one day with this terrible news, saying the doctors thought he may never walk, and if he did it would be with a strange gait. They said he could start having seizures and regress, even if he had progressed for a while. I told Bobby I wouldn't accept that diagnosis, because my God is bigger than all that. And I went to much prayer. After Christopher had learned to walk, he would take off running faster than anyone else could run! I thought surely he would be a fine athlete some day! Today he participates in Special Olympics sports. With God's help, I'm believing he will continue to make progress to be able to be independent later in life.

When my husband was forced, because of certain federal laws governing the State Department, to retire on a Friday in 1995, he was immediately re-hired as a contractor on the following Monday! This was a real blessing in several ways. First, we would no longer have to move overseas. Second, he wouldn't have to travel much, except for an occasional short trip. And also, for the first time in all our years with the Foreign Service, we were finally able to begin saving money, due to his drawing a federal annuity and collecting a good salary at the same time.

When families live overseas in the Foreign Service, they are required to come back to the States for a minimum of six weeks every two years or so. While the government paid our travel costs to and from the States, we had to come up with the money to pay for our family to live somewhere for that length of time. Room and board (usually in motels and restaurants) for a couple with three children, for six weeks in the States, usually cost thousands of dollars. That's why we were never able to get ahead financially over the years. But we always had enough to meet our needs.

When we returned from our first tour in Kenya in 1980, after having lived overseas for ten years, we thought surely I would have to find a job in order to afford to live in the Washington area. But God came through in a miraculous way after my friends and I prayed, and John received two major increases in his salary within our first year back home! I didn't need to go to work after all. I was free to continue to serve the Lord with the Bible Study group God put together. Praise God for all His blessings!

During my time on the Aglow Area Board, I received incredible spiritual and emotional support as I walked through many difficult situations with my family. We had good fellowship and ministry and had such unity of the Spirit most of that time that it was a real joy to serve, even when things might be difficult. I learned how to deal with just about any type of work involved in the Aglow ministry. I even ended up setting up and running the sound system at some of our meetings! I also began doing the retreat flyers and other computer work for our Area Board team.

Sometimes, I would get discouraged by the amount of administrative work, and I would question God about when He was going to let me get back to preaching. I got the sense that all this administrative "stuff" would be necessary in whatever He wanted me to do next! So I could say, "Thank you, Lord, for the training." After about four years as VP of Ministries, I began to experience restlessness and a sense of not being in the right place. I had a feeling I was to be the next President of the Area Board. But the more I saw of what our President did, the less qualified I felt to take over such a position. I tried to "put down" that feeling.

In the fall of 1997, when Alice announced her pending resignation as President, I had a feeling of panic. Believing God wanted me in that position but being afraid of the job is the only way I can describe how I felt. When the day for the election came I didn't even want to be there! But God's will was done and I became the new Area President on the first of January, 1998. It was with much fear and trembling that I took over this position.

CHAPTER NINE

Overcoming Trials

Almost immediately after becoming the President of our Area Leadership Team (a new name for our Area Board), I underwent a baptism in fire, as serious problems came to the forefront in one of our local Aglow groups. I learned very quickly what the Area President has to deal with in terms of difficult personnel issues, and this was one of the most difficult kinds of issues that I've ever seen. God promises wisdom to those who ask and, believe me, I asked. Praise God for godly advisors and regional directors and other leaders in Aglow, who helped me in very difficult circumstances with their great wisdom. And I thank God that His grace is always sufficient in time of need.

On a personal level, I had for many years dealt with several health issues that created a lot of pain. It seemed that almost every tendon and muscle of my body hurt most of the time. My doctor tentatively identified it as fibromyalgia. I went through a course of physical therapy that helped with some areas of pain. I also discovered through various allergy testing that certain allergies caused some of my pain. This helped me to reduce my total levels of discomfort. But still I lived on lots of pain medication.

Then, in the early summer of 1998, my son Bobby began to talk to me about some major problems with his third child, our only granddaughter, Rachel, who was only a month or so of age. She seemed to be blind and deaf! My heart was crushed! After a round of tests, the specialists determined that she, like her older brother Christopher, had microcephaly and developmental delays. The apparent blindness and deafness were not in the eyes or ears themselves, but resulted from the brain's inability to process the information from those organs. We began to pray that God would enable her brain to develop properly in that area. Praise God Rachel can now hear and see, but she still suffers from some (brain-related) visual problems and other developmental delays.

Bobby himself had numerous neurological problems that affected his body in many ways, including temperature regulation, blood pressure fluctuations and heart rate, which seem to have come from a possible bout with Lyme disease in earlier years. Toward the end of September, 1998, I was alarmed when Bobby told me he was having seizures in the middle of the night! Apparently he had sleep apnea, which was depriving his brain of oxygen. Then his brain was not waking him up, as it should, until he went into a seizure, shook himself out of bed, and hit the floor. I urged him to go to a doctor immediately, which he did. Unfortunately, the doctor had not yet arranged for the sleep tests when we received a phone call from his wife Cindy in the wee hours of the morning on October 18, telling us the medics were there working on Bob, and it didn't look good.

Before driving to their house, I called to awaken Alice, my closest friend and spiritual mentor, to pray. I prayed in the Spirit until half way there, when I knew in my heart it was too late. By the time we got there, about 45 minutes after Cindy's call, a neighbor was watching the kids and

Cindy had already left for the hospital with the ambulance. John left me there to stay with the kids and he drove on over to the hospital. I called and woke up my pastor to ask for prayer. It was about 3:00 A.M. on Sunday morning. Before long, the dreaded phone call arrived telling me that our 36-year-old son Bobby had gone to be with the Lord.

I can't begin to describe the depth of pain and grief of losing your child. In those first hours, as my mind was screaming "why?," I knew in my heart that this was God's perfect will for Bobby. He had been in terrible misery physically, emotionally, and spiritually over the past several years. I remembered how (I know it was the Holy Spirit bringing back to my mind), on several occasions, as I had been praying for Bobby, the thought would come that his problems were so overwhelming that he would be better off in heaven. As quickly as that thought (of Bobby dying) would come into my mind, I would immediately cast it out with absolute horror! Bobby himself had made a comment to that effect on the last day I had seen him! Now, in retrospect, I realized God had been trying to prepare me for this time.

I know this sounds strange, but in those wee hours of sleeplessness, I saw very clearly many tangible blessings that would come for Bob's family because of his death. I don't want this to be misunderstood, but I believe this insight came from God, and it came with a peace that passes all understanding. When you know God, then even in the midst of life's worst circumstances you can see His hand working things out for good. He promises that *"in all things God works for the good of those who love Him, who have been called according to His purpose"*(Romans 8:28).

Also, in those hours, God brought to my remembrance a dream or vision Bobby had told me about several years earlier. Neither of us had fully understood this vision. In Bob's vision, he was climbing a mountain, alone, with the city burning behind him. He couldn't understand why his wife and children were not with him in his vision. We both thought, as he related this vision to me, that it had to do with a time of judgment we believed was coming on our nation where cities would be burning, and how God would deliver us. But now, in the hours immediately after Bobby died, I realized his death was the fulfillment of that vision! God would bring this to my remembrance once more many months later at a time when I desperately needed it.

I have learned a great deal over the years about the tactics of our mortal (spiritual) enemy, the devil. But I fell into his trap during my grief by allowing some nagging doubts to come into my mind which threw me into serious torment for several months. In the midst of my grief during those months, I needed God's assurance of Bobby's salvation — that he had gone to heaven.

Two weeks before our own Aglow Area Spring Retreat, five months after Bobby's death, I attended the spring retreat of another Aglow Area, seeking a touch from God. I felt that I could not minister at our own retreat if God didn't minister to me beforehand. On the last morning of this retreat, someone, under the anointing of the Spirit, went to the front and read a Scripture, saying "this is for someone here, but I don't know who." It was a word from the Lord to comfort me. The Scripture was *"Precious in the sight of the Lord is the death of His saints."* (Psalm 116:15) Praise God! I had my assurance — at least for a while.

Bobby had been a genius. He was so smart it frightened me at times. But with that intellect he also had a strange, mischievous sense of humor. He took delight in playing the devil's advocate, without letting us know that was what he was doing! By that I mean he would come out with the most outrageous statements, as though he really believed them, just to see how we would respond! He thought it was very amusing to get a rise out of us on all sorts of issues, many of which were moral or theological. But because he would pretend to be so serious in these statements, it sometimes left me wondering where he really stood on those issues and with God.

The devil again took full advantage of those doubts that had been sown in my mind about whether Bobby really had a relationship with God. He would bring back all those things to my remembrance and begin to torment me with the fear that maybe Bobby hadn't gone to heaven. This went on for several months until I had such grief I could hardly bear it. I cried out to God over and over for some assurance that Bobby was in heaven.

One of those times, before I went to church, I said, "God, I have to know that I know that Bobby is with you!" While I was in church that Sunday morning, the pastor, for some reason, read a Scripture that didn't even seem to fit his sermon. It was the Scripture in Deuteronomy 34 telling how Moses was climbing the mountain where he met with God, saw the Promised Land, then died and was buried by God. The moment I heard that Scripture the Holy Spirit brought back to my mind that vision Bobby had told me of climbing a mountain alone. The same vision that God had reminded me of the night Bobby died! I knew that I knew that I knew, because the Holy Spirit gave me understanding that this was God's answer for me. Bobby had "climbed the mountain" to be with God! God had once more reassured me that Bobby was with Him in heaven. Praise God!

As often happens when one is in the midst of a personal crisis, or struggling with grief, I had failed to remember an important lesson in reference to this situation which was so close to me. Now I had to begin practicing what I had already done in many ways and on many occasions before. I had to begin *"casting down imaginations"*(2 Cor. 10:5 KJV) and *"take captive every thought to make it obedient to Christ"* (2 Cor. 10:5). I had to stop <u>allowing</u> the devil to torment me with all those thoughts and doubts! I had to remember that God had confirmed to me not once, but twice (with Scripture!) that Bobby was a child of God, and therefore was now with Jesus. I had to repent for dwelling on those doubts that came into my mind and accept what God showed me to be the truth.

A few weeks before the time of Bobby's death, I began having a terrible pain in my left shoulder. When I went to my doctor, she thought it was bursitis and gave me a shot of cortisone, which helped immensely, but the relief lasted only a few days. The pain continued to worsen until I suddenly realized with a shock that I was losing mobility in that shoulder!

At that point, in early November, my doctor referred me to a specialist who immediately diagnosed the problem as "Adhesive Capsulitis," commonly called "frozen shoulder." This condition goes through three stages. If not treated with proper physical therapy before all mobility is lost, it can result in permanent disability in that shoulder, or a need for surgery followed by months of therapy. The condition itself is pure agony, and the therapy is even worse. By the time I started therapy, I was already in the second stage, and my shoulder was in such terrible and continuous pain that I could hardly sleep or do anything with that arm.

Therapy consisted of various stretching exercises designed to force the shoulder to do what it didn't want to do, working against the adhesive nature of the disease process in that joint, breaking the adhesions as they formed, so movement could be maintained. Needless to say, this was excruciatingly painful, but, paradoxically, it would give me relief from the pain of the disease for a little while! This exercise regimen took about half an hour to get through and would provide relief for only a few minutes to half an hour before the pain started in again, requiring that the exercises be done again. When I first started therapy, these exercises had to be repeated every half hour or so. Then, gradually, the time between exercise sessions grew longer and longer.

My whole life for at least three months seemed to revolve around this exercise program, which kept my focus on <u>me</u>. That was a miserable time. One day, I was fed up with this endless cycle of pain and the excruciating exercises, followed by relief for a while, followed by pain and more exercises. I cried out to God "Lord, if you don't do something I can't continue to serve in Aglow as president of this Area Team." I told God I was going to quit if he didn't heal me! Then I repented of my anger and frustrations and submitted to His will. Almost immediately, this disease process turned the corner, the pain diminished dramatically, and I rapidly improved!

I know it wasn't my ultimatum to God, but His gracious merciful answer to my heart-cry that brought healing. We can't force God to act by our silly threats. But sometimes we get so consumed by our problems that we lose sight of God and forget Who He is. We fail to praise Him as He deserves. This had been my situation. I was so caught up in focusing on the pain and the exercises that I had lost sight of God and developed a complaining spirit. God hates murmuring and complaining. He commands us in His Word to praise Him in all things. He tells us to offer up a sacrifice of praise. Believe me, when I was in such pain it was indeed a sacrifice to praise God. But now I was finally in a place where I could put my eyes back on God instead of on my endless pain and exercise cycle.

In the normal scheme of things this disease process runs about a year. Mine was over in nine months. I praise God for carrying me through this severe trial of pain and for restoring my shoulder to almost total mobility. And I praise Him for delivering me from the debilitating grief over my son's death which was going on at the same time as my physical torment.

God has also walked me through some other excruciatingly painful treatments for other kinds of pain. These treatments have vastly improved my overall health and enabled me to get off the pain medication. I praise God that He gives doctors the wisdom to find ways to help people. I fully believe in miraculous, divine healing, and have experienced it personally. I know that God has also used me on several occasions to bring healing to others. I would always prefer that God would heal me Himself when I am in pain. But I know that God also uses doctors and medicines. And He sometimes allows pain in our lives for a season to accomplish His own purposes in us.

God says in II Corinthians 1 that He comforts us in all our trials so we may comfort others. As He has brought me through these multiple trials, He has created in me a greater depth of understanding and compassion for those who are suffering than I ever could have had otherwise. I can truly thank God for that. It was often said of Jesus, "*He was moved with compassion.*" If I can't minister with compassion to others, then I will utterly fail to minister like Christ would have me to. In the midst of the worst emotional pain of my life, God has enabled me to feel the pain of others and minister with His compassion. I want to always be "moved with compassion" for those who come to me desiring prayer or other help.

My husband went through a severe trial also, starting with a bad report on his PSA test near the end of 2000. His urologist had been keeping close tabs on this for several years and had done several biopsies over those years as the PSA levels had gradually climbed. But this time the PSA level jumped by more than four points in a few months, so another biopsy was done in January of 2001. This time the report came back as cancer. In February he had surgery to remove his prostate. His recovery went well, and we're praising God for revealing that problem before it went too far.

In and through all of the trials we've experienced in our family, God has trained me for warfare in the spirit realm. Many times He has used me to set people free from demonic oppression. I know it is not me, but God Who is the deliverer! And He lives big in me. I can't tell you how many times over the years people would pour out their problems to me and say, "I don't know why I'm telling you this." It's because God, the Wonderful Counselor, is in me to draw them to Himself and to minister to their needs. It's all God, using me as His vessel, not because I'm special, but because I'm available.

What a marvelous privilege it is to be entrusted with opportunities to share in God's Kingdom work! It has been a wonderful adventure thus far — my getting to know God better! It's exciting beyond measure to experience God working in and through me. I am truly awed by His love and His power to save, heal, and deliver those who come to Him. And I am so grateful that He extended to me the invitation to be part of what He wants to accomplish in this world. My greatest desire is to bring others into His kingdom and to encourage the body of Christ to be over-comers and to be about our Father's business.

God called me many years ago *"to preach good news to the poor, ... to bind up the brokenhearted, to proclaim freedom for the captives, and release from darkness for the prisoners, to proclaim the year of the Lord's favor and the day of vengeance of our God, to comfort all who mourn, and provide for those who grieve in Zion —- to bestow on them a crown of beauty instead of ashes, the oil of gladness instead of mourning, and a garment of praise instead of a spirit of despair"* (Isaiah 61:1-3). He promised to give me the *"treasures of darkness"* (Isaiah 45:3), which I came to understand as souls whom he would use me to deliver from Satan's clutches.

I have already seen God move in many ways on many occasions as I've had the privilege of bringing others to salvation and deliverance, as well as to emotional and physical healing. But I know that I've only just begun to see the fulfillment of His plans and purposes in my life. I'm learning to exercise patience as I await the fulfillment of several prophecies concerning His plans for me. I feel like I'm on the brink of a new exciting explosion of things to do for Him, new ways to serve and bring Him glory! I am eager to see what He will do in days to come!

Appendix

Have you experienced the joy of knowing God has forgiven your sins and made you a part of His family? If so, I pray that this book has stirred in you a desire for an even deeper walk with God, to come to know Him more fully. There's much more to the Christian life than simply enjoying your salvation. Paul said: *"For it is by grace you have been saved, through faith—and this not from yourselves, it is the gift of God— not by works, so that no one can boast. For we are God's workmanship, **created in Christ Jesus to do good works, which God prepared in advance for us to do"** (Ephesians 8:8-10) God calls us to be filled with His Spirit, to walk in obedience to His word, to share His love and the good news of salvation with others, and encourage other believers. You're a part of His body and God wants you to function with the spiritual gifts He has given you to bless others and bring the lost into His kingdom.

If you desire to receive all that He has to give, ask God to forgive your sins, renounce any occult activities that you may have been involved in, and ask Jesus to baptize you in His Holy Spirit.

But if you have discovered, in reading this book, that

you don't really know Him at all or don't have a living relationship with Him, then why not ask Him right now to come into your life? Jesus is the only hope of salvation, the only Way to the Father. There are many religions in the world, but nothing we do or say will ever bring us forgiveness of our sins or give us a relationship with God except confessing our sins to God and believing Jesus died for them. Sin is missing the mark (an archery term) or falling short of God's plan for your life.

The Bible says *"all have sinned and fallen short"* of God's will (Romans 3:23). The Bible says *"the wages of sin is death, but the gift of God is eternal life"* (Romans 6:23). God is holy and righteous and will not look upon sin. Your sin had to be punished. But God loved you so very much that He sent His only begotten Son into the world to pay the penalty for your sin, so that a holy God could offer you forgiveness. Jesus took your punishment in His own body on the cross. But a pardon is useless unless you accept it.

Sin has created a great gulf between you and God. Jesus became the Way to bridge that gulf in order for you to be reconciled to God and become a part of His very own family. God wants to be your Father and to have you as His child. If you've realized you're a sinner and see how sin has separated you from God, and if you desire to know Him in that special relationship of father and child, why don't you pray this prayer right now?

"God, I know I've sinned and made a mess of my life. Please forgive me. I want to experience your love for myself. I believe that Jesus is your Son and that He died for my sin. I believe that you raised Him from the dead and that He's alive today. I ask you to forgive me, take away my sin, and come into my life now and make it new. I accept Jesus Christ as my Savior. I want Him to be Lord of my life. I give myself completely to you. Thank you for

saving me now, in Jesus' name I pray. Amen."

If you prayed this prayer, then you need to tell someone else what you've done. Jesus said if we will confess Him before men, then He will confess us before His heavenly Father. I'd like to hear from you if you want to write. You can contact me through my publisher.

It's also important for you to begin reading the Holy Bible. It's the Word of God and the food your spirit needs in order to grow. I recommend you get a modern translation to help you understand it. I personally like the New International Version. But there are a number of good modern language translations. The New Revised Standard Version, the New American Standard Bible, Today's English Version, and many others are available in most book stores, but especially Christian book stores.

Other people, with the gift of teaching, can help you to understand the difficult parts of the Bible. God gave us teachers for that purpose. But also, the Holy Spirit Who now lives in you will open your mind to understand the Word of God and how it applies to your life. Ask Him to do that every time you sit down to read the Bible.

You also need to find a church near you that preaches and believes the Word of God and get involved in it. This is because you need the support and friendship of fellow believers to encourage you to keep going on the right path. Don't attend a church that says that <u>anything</u> else is <u>equal</u> to the Bible. God's Word, the Holy Bible alone, is all-sufficient to train you in the ways of God and lead you in the way you should go.

May God bless and keep you as you walk through your very own adventures with God, seeking to know Him more fully.

If you wish to contact the author, you may e-mail her a

jwolfpack1@aol.com

or call her at **703-503-2254**